Crisis Assessment and Intervention

COUN 5238

Kanel

CENGAGE
Learning™

Australia • Brazil • Japan • Korea • Mexico • Singapore • Spain • United Kingdom • United States

CENGAGE
Learning·

Crisis Assessment and Intervention: COUN 5238

A Guide to Crisis Intervention, 4th Edition
Kristi Kanel

© 2012 Cengage Learning. All rights reserved.

Executive Editors:
Maureen Staudt
Michael Stranz

Senior Project Development Manager:
Linda deStefano

Marketing Specialist:
Courtney Sheldon

Senior Production/Manufacturing Manager:
Donna M. Brown

PreMedia Manager:
Joel Brennecke

Sr. Rights Acquisition Account Manager:
Todd Osborne

Cover Image:
Getty Images*

*Unless otherwise noted, all cover images used by Custom Solutions, a part of Cengage Learning, have been supplied courtesy of Getty Images with the exception of the Earthview cover image, which has been supplied by the National Aeronautics and Space Administration (NASA).

For product information and technology assistance, contact us at
Cengage Learning Customer & Sales Support, 1-800-354-9706

For permission to use material from this text or product,
submit all requests online at **cengage.com/permissions**
Further permissions questions can be emailed to
permissionrequest@cengage.com

This book contains select works from existing Cengage Learning resources and was produced by Cengage Learning Custom Solutions for collegiate use. As such those adopting and/or contributing to this work are responsible for editorial content accuracy, continuity and completeness.

Compilation © 2011 Cengage Learning.

ISBN-13: 978-1-133-34852-8

ISBN-10: 1-133-34852-1

Cengage Learning
5191 Natorp Boulevard
Mason, Ohio 45040
USA

Cengage Learning is a leading provider of customized learning solutions with office locations around the globe, including Singapore, the United Kingdom, Australia, Mexico, Brazil, and Japan. Locate your local office at:
international.cengage.com/region.
Cengage Learning products are represented in Canada by Nelson Education, Ltd.
For your lifelong learning solutions, visit **www.cengage.com/custom.**
Visit our corporate website at **www.cengage.com.**

Printed in the United States of America

Table of Contents

Ethical and Professional Issues

_____ 1. Professional ethics are based in each state's penal code.

_____ 2. Dual relationships are considered unethical in the counseling profession.

_____ 3. Crisis workers should not engage in a social or business relationship with clients.

_____ 4. Crisis workers may be prone to secondary traumatization.

_____ 5. Crisis workers may suffer burnout due to being emotionally exhausted.

_____ 6. Compassion fatigue occurs when an emergency worker fails to truly care about clients.

_____ 7. Counselors should continuously monitor their countertransference reactions.

_____ 8. Crisis workers must report suicidal ideation to the police.

_____ 9. Confidentiality must be broken if a client is a danger to others.

_____ 10. Continuing education is usually optional for licensed therapists.

The Need for Ethics

Strong ethical practice is especially important in the field of crisis intervention, because clients in crisis come to a counselor in a vulnerable state of disequilibrium and instability. To take advantage of someone in such an unsteady state would be easy. At the outset of counseling, clients often feel hopeless and scared. They may view a counselor who reaches out with empathy with seemingly all the answers as a hero or savior of some type. Crisis interventionists adhere to strong ethical behaviors to help clients see them and their abilities in a realistic light.

Use of Paraprofessionals

As was mentioned prior, some mental health professionals may thinkthat crisis intervention should only be provided by counselors with at least a master's degree or a license. However, as discussed in Chapter 2, crisis intervention began with the use of community workers, sometimes referred to as nonprofessionals or paraprofessionals. These workers often functioned in multidisciplinary team settings such as county agencies and grassroots nonprofit organizations. Effective crisis intervention can be conducted by undergraduate student trainees or community volunteers as well as by graduate-level students and professional counselors if their training is appropriate, and they are properly supervised.

The use of paraprofessional crisis workers has continued to be especially important as the world has moved into the twenty-first century. The economic recession of the early 1990s plus a decided shift in governmental policies during the beginning of the twenty-first century has led to cutbacks in government spending on human services programs, which has meant less money or no money to pay mental health workers. Under these circumstances, the use of volunteers and paraprofessionals makes excellent economic sense because most professional therapists will not provide crisis intervention consistently for the lowered fees often paid to many paraprofessionals. Also, many situations—including the wars in Iraq and Afghanistan, terrorism, continuing experiences of family deterioration, child and spousal abuse, and loss—ensure that crises will be plentiful and intervention desired. When immediate low-cost help is needed, using paraprofessionals makes the community stronger by ensuring that its population is functioning and coping with stress.

Self-Awareness and Countertransference

Therapeutic self-awareness means being conscious of one's own emotions, values, opinions, and behavior. Understanding one's own psychological processes and dynamics can help one guide others through their processes (Corey, Corey, & Callanan, 2010). Students can learn therapeutic self-awareness in crisis intervention classes; such training can help students take an honest, in-depth look at themselves in relation to the crisis of interest. It can be a valuable learning experience, enhancing the crisis worker's skills in helping clients. If workers learn to deal with all the issues surrounding death, for example, they have a better chance of helping a client deal with them.

Countertransference, an issue that must often be addressed in the helping professions, is defined as an "unconsciously determined attitudinal set held by the therapist which interferes with his work" (Singer, 1970, p. 290). Countertransference can be worked through effectively with personal therapy, lab sessions, and active self-exploration. Students new to crisis intervention have often experienced one or more of the situational crises practiced in coaching sessions. If students have not worked through the crisis completely, their feelings may interfere with their ability to remain calm, objective, and client-focused. However, once students' unresolved issues are discovered and processed, both in their own counseling and in lab group, they often are able to work quite effectively with clients going through that same type of crisis. Countertransference is not restricted to students in training. In actuality, this concept was first developed by Carl Jung in his training of analysts. Even the highly trained professional is liable to experience countertransference from time to time. This is the primary reason that personal analysis has been encouraged for psychoanalysts from the very beginning of the discipline.

Dual Relationships

Another ethical issue involves **dual relationships**—that is, a counselor's having more than one kind of relationship with a client. When counselors are providing crisis intervention to a client, they are prohibited from being involved with that client on a personal level of any kind. This includes prohibition of any relationship—sexual, social, employment, or financial—that is not directly related to the provision of crisis intervention. Such a separation is necessary because a person in crisis is often in a vulnerable state and could be taken advantage of quite easily by a counselor (who is viewed as an expert). Another reason to avoid a dual relationship is because of the possible emotional damage clients may sustain if they experience the counselor in a different role and then are disillusioned or disappointed. Also, the power differential between counselor and client is enormous. The counselor knows quite a bit about the client, and this knowledge can be a source of awkwardness for the client when he or she is out of the therapeutic situation. The most potent word on the subject is this: *Don't make friends or lovers of your clients. It is unethical and in some cases illegal.*

Confidentiality

Confidentiality is one of the hallmarks of any trusting relationship. It is also an important part of the ethical code for mental health providers. A broad concept that refers to safeguarding clients from unauthorized disclosures of information made in the therapeutic relationship, confidentiality is an explicit promise by the counselor to reveal nothing unless the client has agreed to it. **Privileged communication**, which is sometimes confused with confidentiality, is the statutory right that protects clients from having their confidences revealed publicly (Corey, Corey, & Callanan, 2010).

However, some exceptions to privilege and confidentiality do exist, as they relate to crisis intervention. Privilege is waived if the client signs a document giving the helper permission to disclose the communications between the client and the counselor. Clients may be asked to waive privilege to ensure continuity of care among mental health professionals, to provide for appropriate supervision when access to records is needed for court testimony, and when information is needed for submitting health insurance claims. Confidentiality must be broken in cases of child abuse or elder abuse, when clients are a danger to others, and it may be broken when clients are a danger to themselves or are gravely disabled. Sometimes, a client's mental condition will be the focus of a lawsuit, and in some of those cases confidentiality can be ethically and legally broken. For example, a client who sues a therapist for malpractice and claims to have suffered emotional damage because of the therapist's incompetence gives up privileged communications from the therapy sessions. The therapist may use case notes to defend against the malpractice charge. A similar example in which a client would forfeit the protection of privilege is a case in which the client is attempting to prove emotional injury in a workers' compensation lawsuit.

In order to remember these exceptions to confidentiality, the following philosophy offered by Justice Mathew O. Tobriner of the California Supreme Court, after the court heard *Tarasoff v Regents of the University* and created the duty to warn mandate, is often applied: "Privileged communication ends where public peril begins." (Buckner & Firestone, 2000). This includes peril to clients if they endanger themselves because of a mental disorder. If clients are considered suicidal or gravely disabled and unable to care for themselves, helpers may breach confidentiality to protect them. The spirit of this allowance is that sharing information is meant to be among professionals, family, and friends, and not for frivolous purposes. Gravely disabled clients are those who, because of a mental disorder, cannot take care of their daily needs for food, shelter, medical care, clothing, and so on. Clearly, it is more important to break confidentiality to save someone with Alzheimer's disease from starving because he is delusional about having food in the house than it is to maintain confidentiality.

The other situations in which privileged communications should be broken involve trying to prevent clients from harming others. These conditions include elder abuse, child abuse, and the possibility that clients might cause different kinds of danger to others. Specifics of mandatory reporting are presented next.

Elder Abuse Reporting Act

The department of social services in some states has an adult protective services program that responds to reports of abuse of the elderly (i.e., adults over 65 years old). Elder abuse refers to any of the following acts inflicted by other than accidental means on an elder by another person: physical abuse, fiduciary abuse (involves trust and money), and neglect or abandonment. In many states, knowledge of such abuse must be reported to social services, the police, or a nursing home ombudsman (governmental investigator). Some agencies have also begun taking reports of abuse of the disabled adult population. This could cover any adult who suffers from a mental or physical disability such as mental retardation or blindness.

Child Abuse Reporting Act

Since passage by Congress of the National Child Abuse Prevention and Treatment Act in 1974, many states have enacted laws requiring professionals to report child abuse. This act provided federal funding to states in support of prevention, assessment, investigation, prosecution, and treatment activities. It was amended several times and was most recently amended and reauthorized in 2003 by the Keeping Children and Families Safe Act (P.L. 108-36) (U.S. Department of Health and Human Services, 2010). States differ on the indicators for reporting and whether sanctions will be imposed on individuals for not reporting. Child abuse reporting includes suspicions of physical abuse, sexual abuse, general neglect, and emotional abuse.

In many states, child abuse must be reported within 36 hours of its discovery to the department of social services or the police. The child protective services program will then investigate the suspicion. Remember that there is no requirement to have evidence of abuse before it can be reported; suspicion alone is enough evidence. If abuse is suspected that is later proved, and it is not reported, there may be fines by the state. On the other hand, more and more states are ensuring immunity from suit for false reports. Each crisis worker is encouraged to know the requirements of reporting in his or her state.

The Tarasoff Case   The consequences of failing to warn an individual of possible danger to her or him by another are dramatically illustrated in the Tarasoff case. In 1969, Prosenjit Poddar was seeing a therapist at the campus counseling center of the University of California, Berkeley. Poddar confided to the therapist that he intended to kill Tatiana Tarasoff when she returned from Brazil. The therapist considered Poddar dangerous and called campus police, requesting that Poddar be confined. He was not confined. To complicate matters, the therapist's supervisor ordered that all case notes be destroyed. Tarasoff was later killed by Poddar, and her parents filed suit against the California Board of Regents. The decision from this case requires a therapist to notify the police and the intended victim when possible if the therapist has reasonable belief that a client is dangerous toward others (duty to warn) (California State Case Law, 2010).

Informed consent is a way of providing clients with information they need to become active participants in the therapeutic relationship (Corey, Corey, & Callanan, 2010). Although no specific rules exist governing how much information a therapist is to provide, three legal elements to informed consent do exist. First, clinicians must make sure clients have the ability to make rational decisions and, if not, must ensure that a parent or guardian takes responsibility for giving consent. Second, therapists must give clients information in a clear way and check their understanding of the risks and benefits of treatment and alternate procedures available. Third, clients must consent freely to treatment. The exceptions to these elements occur when clients are dangerous to themselves and others or are gravely disabled. Electroconvulsive shock treatments and psychosurgery (lobotomies) cannot be done without consent; however, there are times when medication is given without client consent.

Supervision and Training

The ethical code requiring counselors to receive appropriate supervision and training must be followed for both the benefit of the client and the clinician's growth and confidence. Unless paraprofessionals are supervised by a licensed professional, most agencies—county, state, and nonprofit—do not let them provide crisis intervention and counseling. Even seasoned therapists often consult with colleagues about cases for which they have minimal training or experience. Referring a client to another helper is sometimes done by crisis workers, because the worker's duties mainly involve assessment and brokering out clients—tasks requiring a sound knowledge of community resources for a variety of problems.

Being able to make an assessment for organic illnesses and severe mental illness is especially important when a helper is conducting a crisis interview. Some cases require a multidisciplinary team approach with medical doctor involvement; any serious mental illness or neurological impairment must be identified if the patient is to receive the total help needed. Even though making technical diagnoses is not usually considered appropriate for paraprofessionals, knowledge of the *Diagnostic and Statistical Manual of Mental Disorders* IV-TR (American Psychiatric Association, 2000) is helpful in ensuring that clients receive services from the type of professional appropriate to their needs. This manual provides information about very serious mental disorders that require intervention by physicians. Crisis workers should review this manual when possible to gain a beginning understanding of the types of presenting complaints that usually necessitate physician involvement. Chapter 5 describes how to use the Mental Status Exam to determine whether a client suffers from serious mental health conditions and therefore would need to be referred to a physician.

Box 3.1   Example of an Organic Illness Necessitating Physician Intervention

Suppose that a 45-year-old woman comes to a community center because her 70-year-old mother has been behaving strangely, does not recognize her family members, and leaves the gas stove burners on all day. Knowing that these symptoms are indicative of Alzheimer's disease or other organic brain disorders helps the crisis worker develop treatment strategies. Most important is having the mother examined neurologically to rule out any medical cause for her unusual behavior.

Multicultural Competence

The idea that counselors should be sensitive to various cultural norms and behaviors when helping clients work through crises is nearly universally accepted. Crisis workers are encouraged to be open and knowledgable towards subgroups that may differ from mainstream culture. Counselors must not impose personal values on clients, but instead listen to how their values may be a part of the problems that exist. Of course, one can't help but sometimes expose one's values to others, but it is considered unethical to assume that everyone should believe and act the way counselors think they should.

This notion of multicultural competence is considered so important that an entire chapter is devoted to multicultural issues and interventions (see Chapter 6).

Burnout and Secondary Posttraumatic Stress Disorder

People who regularly work with individuals in crisis situations may be prone to develop symptoms of burnout, or what can be referred to as secondary post-traumatic stress disorder (PTSD), which will be covered in detail in Chapter 9.

Burnout has been studied by many and has been seen in a variety of workers throughout the nation. Crisis workers should be informed about the possible symptoms and causes of burnout to be able to identify this state in themselves. The causes, definitions, and prevention of burnout are discussed. Secondary PTSD, or secondary traumatization, is then discussed in the context of a research study conducted by the author with 67 community workers who deal with crisis situations daily.

Definitions of Burnout

Maslach and Jackson (1986) have proposed three dimensions of burnout. Lack of personal accomplishment, emotional exhaustion, as well as depersonalization and deindividuation of clients are often the reactions of workers to chronic stress. Burnout can be thought of as a "syndrome of physical and emotional exhaustion involving the development of negative self-concept, negative job attitudes, and a loss of concern and feelings for clients" (Pines & Maslach, 1978, p. 224). When these reactions occur, individuals in the helping professions who are particularly susceptible to burnout may develop negative and cynical attitudes and feelings toward clients and may not be as supportive as needed (Vettor & Kosinski, 2000, p. 1).

Symptoms of Burnout

Researchers have described a variety of physical and emotional symptoms indicative of burnout. In the 1980s, hundreds of workers at an aircraft manufacturing facility developed symptoms of burnout that were referred to as aerospace syndrome. Most suffered from dizziness, nausea, headaches, fatigue, palpitations, shortness of breath, and cognitive impairment. Three-fourths of them also showed symptoms of major depression and panic disorder (Sparks et al., 1990).

Other common symptoms of burnout include psychosomatic illness, social withdrawal, substance abuse, and deterioration of family and social relationships (Freudenberger, 1975; Maslach & Jackson, 1986).

Causes of Burnout

Negative emotional and behavioral reactions on the job occur in many professions. Human service workers may be more prone to burnout as a result of conflicts between an idealistic "professional mystique" and the harsh realities of working in human services (Leiter, 1991). In addition, human services workers may find it emotionally taxing when consumers resent them, when they must work with consumers with limited capabilities to help themselves, when they must deal with tedious bureaucratic exercises daily, and when they receive little positive feedback from authority figures (Gomez & Michaelis, 1995). Lack of company support, poor relations among staff, lack of competence, and a perception that success is unlikely on the job are other general causes of burnout (Clarke, 2000).

In helping professions in which the professionals such as emergency medical technicians (EMTs) must deal with intense emotional arousal, depersonalization is used to minimize this arousal. Burnout may be seen as a coping strategy to ensure that performance is not affected in these crisis situations. Burnout may also occur as part of a tendency for helping professionals to evaluate themselves negatively when assessing their work with patients (Vettor & Kosinski, 2000). EMTs may be more susceptible to burnout because they are faced with human tragedies such as as injury, mutilation, and death on a daily basis. Services are often delivered in a hostile world of darkness, poor weather conditions, difficult terrain, and unpredictable dangers (Vettor & Kosinski, 2000). The technicians are at risk for developing secondary PTSD from exposure to critical incidents. (Effects of exposure to critical incidents are discussed in detail in Chapter 9.)

Negative emotional and behavioral reactions have also been observed in professionals who are not considered to be in the helping professions but who deal with crisis situations. Aerospace syndrome was determined to be caused by several psychosocial aspects in the workplace. Fear of chemicals, labeling of aerospace syndrome, fear of AIDS, mass hysteria crisis building, work intensity, mental strain, increased production pressure, tense labor-management relations, inadequate attention to safety, and reinforcement of fear by media and coworkers were all found to be causes of high work-stress burnout among aerospace workers (Vettor & Kosinski, 2000). The mass hysteria was so extreme that only 14 of the hundreds of workers observed showed no symptoms!

Several conditions may help prevent burnout and increase positive emotional reactions among workers. Kruger, Bernstein, and Botman (1995) suggest that having fun with team members, work discussions, peer cohesion, and social support, in which assistance is directed toward helping the worker cope with stressful circumstances, combine to reduce symptoms of burnout.

Human services workers who spend more time in direct contact with consumers and less time processing paperwork had higher scores on personal accomplishment assessments (Gomez & Michaelis, 1995). Reduced feelings of personal accomplishment have been associated with burnout, so it appears that one way to reduce burnout would be to spend more time with clients. However, because paperwork is often required in human services occupations, management would be wise to ensure that workers have enough client contact, as this seems to buffer workers against the worst effects of stress and is a valuable source of reward among staff. Other factors that may reduce burnout include workers feeling that they have some control over their time at work, some control over their workload, and an ability to organize their own work. Recognition of quality of care is also helpful in reducing burnout, as is clarity over one's role at work.

Secondary Traumatic Stress

A particular type of burnout might be thought of as secondary trauma stress or compassion fatigue (Collins & Long, 2003) and is sometimes referred to as secondary traumatic stress disorder (Figley, 1995). Too much exposure to serious illness or crisis states might create feelings of depression and learned helplessness in a helper. Demanding case loads and long hours might precipitate these feelings. When a crisis worker deals with trauma daily, they might experience vicarious stress or trauma (Bride, 2004), that is, absorbing the trauma from the victims that they help. This leads us to accept that "mental health workers are vulnerable to physical and psychological consequences when dealing with the traumatic life event of others (Marcus & Dubi, 2006, p. 223). Figley (1995) suggests that this vulnerability is a natural consequence that results from listening to others speak about traumatizing events, and that the level of distress experienced by the mental health worker depends on the characteristics of the helper and of the the client population.

These characteristics of the mental health worker were studied by Marcus and Dubi (2006). They were interested in whether a counselor's personal trauma history, particularly from their childhood, was a significant risk factor in that counselors developed secondary trauma syndrome. They used several instruments such as the Compassion Satisfaction and Fatigue Test, the Trauma Recovery Scale, Burns Anxiety Inventory, and Burns Depression Checklist to assess compassion satisfaction, burnout, and compassion fatigue among 197 professional counselors, graduate counseling students, and other mental health workers. Their findings indicate no significant relationship between compassion fatigue and prior personal trauma.

Another Study of Community Crisis Workers as Related to Secondary PTSD and Burnout

Sixty-seven community workers were surveyed in 2001 by the author with the assistance of several of her students who collected data by personally distributing questionnaires to various community workers experiencing frequent work with crisis situations. These workers responded to questions regarding their emotional and behavioral reactions to working with people in crisis. Emergency room physicians and nurses, ambulance drivers, mental health workers, rape crisis counselors, firefighters, and police were included. The types of crisis situations they commonly work with were also identified.

Of the 67 workers surveyed, 21 identified themselves as counselors or therapists, 12 as police officers, 3 as physicians, 11 as nurses, 5 as emergency response workers, 7 as firefighters, and 8 as "other."

Table 3.1 shows the types of crises dealt with according to occupation.

TABLE 3.1   Types of Crises Dealt with by Occupation

Type of Crisis Situation	Counselor	Police	Physician	Nurse	Emergency Response Worker	Firefighter	Other
	N = 21	N = 12	N = 3	N = 11	N = 5	N = 7	N = 8
Medical	4	12	3	11	4	3	0
Sexual assault	12	7	1	8	3	5	6
Spousal abuse	17	8	2	7	2	6	7
Child abuse	19	7	1	7	2	6	4
Victim of robbery or burglary	1	3	0	7	1	5	1
Victim of physical assault	14	7	2	10	4	6	5
Significant other of a murder victim	1	3	0	4	1	5	0
Victim of a natural disaster	1	2	0	7	3	4	0
Victim of a shooting spree	1	3	1	7	3	3	0
Substance abuse crisis	6	11	3	9	3	5	3
Sexually transmitted disease, HIV, AIDS crisis	5	6	2	9	2	3	1
Teen runaway, pregnancy, disobedience	16	4	2	2	1	4	6
Disability crisis	5	9	2	8	3	2	2
Illness crisis	8	11	3	9	4	2	2

The participants were asked several questions about their reactions to working with people in crisis. When asked if they felt anxiety when a client reports being suicidal, 23 (34%) of the crisis workers said yes. Only 12 (17%) reported being depressed after working with a person in crisis. However, when asked if there had ever been times when the worker was unable to stop thinking about clients in crisis, 41 (64%) said yes. These problems do not seem to prevent workers from going to work, though, as only 1% of all counselors said they had missed work as a result of working with people in crisis. There was little increase in drug or alcohol use reported as a result of working with crises. Only five people stated that their use increased. This low number does not mean that the workers do not feel stress. In response to the question about feeling powerless after working with people in crisis, 23 (34%) answered that they did. This same percentage stated that they felt grouchy or agitated after dealing with people in crisis.

One common response of workers who deal with crises seems to be anger at the system. Thirty (45%) stated feeling angry at the system when working with someone in crisis. It is no wonder then that 35 (52%) of the workers stated that they think of quitting their job one to five times a month.

As to what these workers do when feeling emotionally stressed after working with people in crisis, the vast majority (80%) stated they talk with coworkers. Only 13 (19%) stated that they seek professional mental health services when feeling emotionally stressed.

The results of this study and previously discussed studies indicate that workers have many emotional, psychological, and behavioral reactions to stressful working conditions. In the case of crisis workers, many of the symptoms reported in this study are similar to the types of symptoms found in people going through a crisis. Symptoms of posttraumatic stress disorder included the inability to stop thinking about the client in crisis, agitation, irritability, anxiety, depression, and thoughts of wanting to quit the job. Because these symptoms are a result of working with people going through a crisis and not the result of the workers' own personal crises, it can be thought of as **secondary PTSD** *or* **secondary traumatization.**

The fact that these symptoms were reported to exist by so many of the surveyed crisis workers indicates a need for a strategy to reduce these symptoms. As was shown in many of the studies presented earlier, as well as in the responses of this current study, maintaining ongoing communication with coworkers is essential in managing the symptoms. It is hoped that this will allow crisis workers to stay on the job at peak effectiveness.

A very recent case (November, 2009) of extreme burnout and secondary traumatization occurred when a military psychiatrist shot and killed over 10 people at Fort Hood. As of the writing of this text, officials are still trying to determine whether he committed these killings due to religious/terrorist reasons or as a result of listening to soldiers describe their experiences in Iraq and Afghanistan, with the possibility that he too would soon be deployed to Iraq.

Chapter Review

Ethics are guidelines of acceptable behaviors within a profession, usually determined by those in the profession themselves. The counseling profession has very specific standards regarding confidentiality, dual relationships, mandatory reporting of abuse, informed consent, and counselor training and supervision. Because clients are thought to be vulnerable, counselors adhere to these standards to protect clients from being exploited. Part of being in a helping profession is to monitor ones own emotional well-being. Crisis workers may be prone to developing burnout and secondary traumatization because of their daily contact with people suffering trauma. Crisis counselors can deal with these issues by engaging in ongoing dialogues with colleagues and by seeking their own counseling when necessary.

Correct Answers to Pre-Chapter Quiz

F 2. T 3. T 4. T 5. T 6. F 7. T 8. F 9. T 10. F

Key Terms for Study

burnout: Feelings and behaviors that often result when a crisis worker feels powerless to help people in crisis. Symptoms of burnout include absenteeism, agitation, depression, anxiety, and anger.

child abuse reporting: Reporting required of anyone working with children as a counselor, doctor, teacher, or any other capacity since passage of the 1974 Child Abuse Prevention and Treatment Act by Congress. These people must report any suspicions of child abuse to the child protective services agency in their state. The requirement is mandatory and in many states overrides the client's right to confidentiality.

confidentiality: An ethical standard providing the client with the right for all disclosures in counseling to be kept private.

countertransference: A situation in a counseling relationship that arises from unresolved feelings experienced by a counselor in a session with a client. These feelings come out of the counselor's personal life and cause him or her to act out these feelings with a client, behavior that may cause emotional harm to the client.

danger to others: Condition in which a client is deemed to be a threat to others. At this time, the counselor must breach confidentiality and report his or her concerns to the police or the intended victim, or both. This is called the "duty to warn."

dual relationship: A relationship that a counselor engages in with the client outside the professional one—for example, a social, sexual, or business relationship.

elder abuse: Physical abuse, fiduciary abuse, neglect, or abandonment of someone 65 years old or older. In many states, anyone working with clients over 65 years of age must report suspected cases of elder abuse to the state's adult protective services agency. This reporting is often mandatory and grounds for breaching confidentiality.

exceptions to privilege and confidentiality: Situations in which communications between therapist and client can be legally and ethically shared with others. In the case of confidentiality, these include elder abuse and child abuse; when the client is gravely disabled; and when the client is a danger to self or others. In the case of privilege, these include voluntary waivers given by the client for information to be shared in a limited forum as well as some involuntary disclosure, as in certain court cases.

gravely disabled: Condition in which clients are psychotic or suffering from a severe organic brain disorder. People with such disorders are often incapable of meeting basic needs, such as obtaining food or shelter and managing finances. Being gravely disabled is often a reason for involuntary hospitalization of a person.

informed consent: Permission for treatment given by a client to a therapist after the client has been thoroughly informed about all aspects of the treatment. Anyone entering a counseling relationship has the right to understand the nature of therapy, give his or her consent for it, understand that it is voluntary, and be told the limits of confidentiality.

Mental Status Exam: An examination used to rule out severe forms of mental illness and organic disorders. As part of their ethical responsibility, crisis interventionists must know when to refer a client to a physician. Use of this exam can help in making those determinations.

Privileged communication: The legal counterpart of confidentiality. Clients may waive the right to privilege if they wish the counselor to share certain information in court or other limited venues.

Secondary PTSD/Traumatization: When a crisis worker suffers emotional and behaviorally after working with clients in crisis.

The ABC Model of Crisis Intervention

_____ 1. Basic attending skills help develop and maintain contact.

_____ 2. Reflection of feelings is contraindicated for clients in crisis.

_____ 3. It is usually best to ask a series of close-ended questions during crisis intervention.

_____ 4. The ABC model of crisis intervention tends to have more structure than long term therapy.

_____ 5. Educational statements provide clients with information about their situation.

_____ 6. Crisis workers try to identify the precipiating event, perceptions, and impairments in functioning.

_____ 7. Validation statements let clients know that the counselor approves of their decisions.

_____ 8. In the coping phase, the counselor tells the client what to do.

_____ 9. Twelve-step groups are a great resource because they are readily available and free.

_____ 10. Clients in crisis should not be expected to come up with ideas about how to improve their situation.

Introduction

The ABC model of crisis intervention is a method for conducting very brief mental health interviews with clients whose functioning level has decreased following a psychosocial stressor. This model follows the formula presented in Chapter 1 regarding the process of crisis formation. It is a problem-focused approach and is most effectively applied within four to six weeks of the stressor. Identifying the cognitions of the client as they relate to the precipitating event and then altering them to help decrease unmanageable feelings is the central focus of the method. In addition, providing community referrals and other **resources** such as reading material is also essential in applying this model.

Caplan and Lindemann first conceptualized the crisis intervention approach in the 1940s (Caplan, 1964; Lindemann, 1944) while others have since developed models that use the principles and techniques of these founders. The ABC model of crisis intervention presented in this text has its origins in a variety of sources. It is loosely based on Jones's (1968) A-B-C method of crisis management, with its three-stage process: A, achieving contact; B, boiling the problem down to basics; and C, coping. Moline (1986), a former professor at California State University, Fullerton, developed a course called Crisis Intervention, in which she used a modified version of Jones's model. From her lecture notes and from discussions with her about how she organized the course, the author developed, as noted in Chapter 2, the ABC model of crisis intervention discussed in this book. Over a period of 24 years, the author has expanded and revised the ABC model. Revisions are based on current information from experts in the community who provide crisis intervention for a variety of populations, the author's experiences in teaching the model to students and community counselors, and receiving feedback from these students, and the author's experiences as a counselor in public, private, and nonprofit agency settings.

Other models have also influenced the ABC model of crisis intervention in terms of the particular structure and stages. Structuring the counseling process around certain phases or stages is not a new phenomenon. It has been done by mental health practitioners since the days of such founding theorists as Sullivan (1954) and Adler (Corey, 2008). The structure of Adlerian counseling follows four central objectives that corresponds to four phases. These phases do not progress in rigid steps but are best understood as a weaving that leads to a tapestry (Dreikurs, 1967). The phases that Adler developed are:

1. Establishing the Relationship
2. Exploring Indiviudal Psychologica Dynamics
3. Encouraging Self-Understanding and Insight
4. Reorientation and Reeducation.

These four phases are similar to those of the ABC model:

FIGURE 4.1   The ABC Model as Related to Adler's Four-Phase Model here

   A. Developing and maintaining contact (corresponds with Adler's phase 1)
   B. Identifying the problem and providing therapeutic interaction (corresponds with Adler's phase 2 and phase 3)
   C. Coping (corresponds with Adler's phase 4)

Sullivan (1954) also used a phase model to structure psychiatric interviews. His stages can also be viewed as corresponding with the stages of the ABC model: Phase 1, the formal inception (analogous to A of the ABC model); Phase 2, the reconnaissance, and Phase 3, the detailed inquiry (analogous to B); and Phase 4, termination (analogous to C).

Although the ABC model of crisis intervention has a three-stage approach, in an actual interview the components of any one stage could be used at any time. Readers are strongly encouraged to keep this thought in mind during the discussion of each stage that follows. The crisis worker will learn how to integrate the stages through practice and experience.

A: Developing and Maintaining Rapport

The foundation of crisis intervention is the development of **rapport**—a state of understanding and comfort—between client and counselor. As a client begins to feel rapport, trust and openness follow, allowing the interview to proceed. Before delving into the client's personal world, the counselor must achieve this personal contact. The counseling relationship is unique in this regard; before any work can be done, the client must feel understood and accepted by the counselor. A student of the author summed up this need quite appropriately: "People don't care what you know, until they know that you care."

By learning several basic attending skills, the beginning crisis counselor can develop the self-confidence needed to make contact with someone in crisis. Use of these basic rapport-building communication skills invites clients to talk, brings calm control to the situation, allows them to talk about the facts of the situation, helps the counselor to hear and empathize with the client's feelings, and lets the client know that the counselor is concerned and respectful. Remember that the interview process does not proceed in a linear fashion; the various attending skills can be interwoven as appropriate. For example, the counselor may ask a question before reflecting or may reflect before asking a question.

Unlike other approaches to counseling, crisis intervention does not typically include the use of such techniques as interpretation or direct advice giving. These techniques generally require a therapeutic relationship of long duration before they are effective; in crisis intervention, developing such a relationship is not practical. Although it may be tempting to jump in and tell clients what is wrong with them and what to do about it, the crisis interventionist is encouraged not to do this. The basic attending skills are a useful alternative to the sometimes rote practice of asking routine questions and giving routine advice and interpretations.

The primary purpose of using the basic attending skills is to gain a clear understanding of the internal experience of the crisis as the client sees it. Only when the counselor truly understands can he or she help to bring change to the client's subjective distress and assist the client in improving his or her functioning.

Table 4.1 can be used as a guide for the beginning counselor. It is not meant to be followed as a linear script but rather as a reminder of the skills the counselor is to use throughout the interview. Skill proficiency columns are built into the table to allow evaluation of student performance by the course instructor.

Attending Behavior

The most basic skill of helping is listening. Appropriate verbal and nonverbal behavior—that is, **attending behavior**—is the hallmark of a helping interview. Good eye contact, attentive body language, expressive vocal style, and verbal following are valuable listening tools, but they are not always present. The next time you carry on a conversation with a friend, observe whether these behaviors are in evidence. Using a soft, soothing voice, showing an interested face, having relaxed posture, leaning toward the client, making direct eye contact, and maintaining close physical proximity (Cormier et al., 1986, p. 30) are all ways to convey warmth and are part of active listening. These attending behaviors "demonstrate to the client that you are with him or her and indeed are listening," enabling the client to talk more freely (Ivey, Gluckstern, & Ivey, 1997, p. 19).

Active listening requires being able to observe the client and at the same time pay attention to how one should best react to the client. Try the following exercise presented in Box 4.1.

Crisis workers must remember that the attending behavior of different cultural and ethnic groups may vary in style, and these helpers may need to adapt when working with various sub- groups (special issues related to sub-groups will be discussed later in the book). Ivey and colleagues (1997, pp. 20–21) have summarized typical variations:

- *Eye Contact:* African Americans, Latin Americans, and Native Americans may avoid eye contact as a sign of respect. With Latinos, direct sustained eye contact can represent a challenge to authority. A bowed head may be a sign of respect from Native Americans.
- *Body Language:* The public behavior of African Americans may seem emotionally intense and demonstrative to European Americans. A slap on the back may be insulting to an Asian American or a Latin American.
- *Vocal Style:* Latin Americans often begin meetings with lengthy greetings and pleasant talk before addressing key issues. European Americans tend to value a quiet, controlled vocal style; other groups may see this as manipulative or cold.

TABLE 4.1   Basic Attending Skills

	Skill Proficiency		
	Good	Fair	Poor
Attending behavior			
Eye contact			
Warmth			
Body posture			
Vocal style			
Verbal following			
Overall empathy			
(focus on client)			
Questioning			
Open-ended			
Close-ended			
Paraphrasing			
Restating in own words			
Clarifying			
A close-ended question that serves to clarify what the client just said			
Reflection			
Painful feelings			
Positive feelings			
Ambivalent feelings			
Nonverbal feelings			
Summarization			
Tying together precipitating event, subjective distress, and cognitive elements			

Source: From Basic Attending Skills, Third Edition, by A. E. Ivey, N. B. Gluckstern, and M. B. Ivey, pp. 19, 20–21, 35, 56, and 92. Copyright © 1997 Microtraining Associates. Reprinted with permission.

- *Verbal Following:* Asian Americans may prefer a more indirect and subtle communication and consider the African American or European American style too direct and confrontational. Personal questions may be especially offensive to Native Americans.

Box 4.1   Basic Attending Behaviors Exercise

Break into groups of three or four. Using the basic attending skills evaluation sheet in Table 4.1, rate each other on attending behaviors. One person can play the client and another can be a crisis worker. A third can be the rater. The rater also enhances her or his skills of observation while giving feedback to the counselor. After this exercise, have some fun exaggerating an interview in which the crisis worker does not employ these behaviors (i.e., has poor eye contact, is cold, keeps arms folded, does not pay attention verbally). This behavior will impress on everyone what not to do!

Questioning

Asking clients pertinent questions is an invitation to them to talk. **Open-ended questions** provide room for clients to express their real selves without categories imposed by the interviewer. They allow clients an opportunity to explore their thoughts and feelings with the support of the interviewer. **Close-ended questions** can help the interviewer gather factual information such as age or marital status. However, clients frequently feel attacked or defensive with certain close-ended questions (such as "why" "do you" "are you" "have you" and "did you" questions), which should be used sparingly if at all (Ivey et al., 1997, p. 35).

Beginning counseling students tend to ask "do you, have you, could you, and would you" questions. These types of close-ended questions can be answered with a "yes" or "no" by clients, with the result of a bogged-down interview. Counselors might try to avoid these types of close-ended questions, asking more specific open-ended questions instead.

Try to tie your open-ended questions to what the client has just said. Questions that begin with "what" and "how" are very effective in allowing the client to explore his or her ideas and feelings. When the question is posed effectively, it helps move the interview along and allows gathering essential information about the nature of the crisis. Remember, it is effective and appropriate to ask pointed open-ended questions when they relate to what the client has just said, and, hence, verbal following is extremely important to proper questioning. Whenever a client offers a new word or expresses energy behind what he or she says, the counselor can ask a question that helps him or her to better understand the meaning of the word or the energy. Never assume that you know what the client means. Inquire!

The following dialogue between a client and a crisis worker shows an appropriate use of questions.

CLIENT: "I am so angry at my husband. He won't talk to me anymore and we just don't communicate at all."

CRISIS WORKER: "What do you mean by communicate?"

CLIENT: "He refuses to sit down and listen to me. I have no idea what his problem is. I can't get him to tell me anything. He obviously doesn't want to be around, but I don't know why."

CRISIS WORKER: "What makes you think he doesn't want to be around?"

CLIENT: "He is never home. He stays late at work, out with his friends every night, and is gone on the weekends. I don't know how long I can stand it."

CRISIS WORKER: "What do you mean by you don't know how long you can stand it?"

CLIENT: "Well, I am crying every night, my kids wonder where their dad is, and I am miserable and don't want to live like this."

(At this point, a reflection of feelings would be helpful, as would some close-ended questions about the kids' ages.)

Of course, these are not the only questions that could be asked. But notice that each question relates to what the client has just said, which has the effect of unrolling the client's cognitive and emotional experience. A useful metaphor is to think of the client's cognitive schema as a tree. The client presents the counselor with the trunk in the beginning. As the interview progresses, there is movement up the trunk and onto the branches. Each question allows movement onto the smaller branches and twigs, until the entire tree has been explored and is viewed in its totality. All branches, twigs, and leaves are connected to the trunk, whether directly or indirectly. When the counselor can see the tree fully, the nature of the crisis can be fully understood, and movement into offering coping strategies and altering cognitions can be accomplished.

Below are some examples of poorly worded questions and appropriately worded questions.

Poorly Worded Counselor Questions	Appropriately Worded Counselor Questions
Do you feel sad about losing your husband?	How do you feel about losing your husband?
Have you tried to talk to your father?	What have you done?
Could you tell me more about your sadness?	What is your sadness like for you?

Providing information in response to open-ended questions is generally more comfortable for clients than giving answers to 20 close-ended intake questions. There is a time and place for close-ended questions, usually when a fact is needed and during suicide assessments. Although it is true that many counselors must complete forms for their agencies, this does not mean that the interview should be a series of close-ended questions. Interweaving close-ended questions with open-ended questions, reflection, and paraphrasing usually allows a counselor to complete intake forms in most agencies. This takes practice, but clients benefit from this style.

Following are some examples of effective open-ended and close-ended questions. Included are suggestions for changing "why" questions into open-ended questions. Role-play these questions with friends.

Effective Open-Ended Questions	Appropriate Close-Ended Questions
How have you been feeling?	How long have you been married?
What is the worst part for you of being raped?	Have you been checked by a doctor yet?
What is it like for you to be diagnosed with AIDS?	Are you taking any medications?
How are you doing at work lately?	How old are your children?
What are your thoughts about death?	Has your husband ever abused the kids?
	Are you thinking of hurting yourself?

"Why" Questions	Open-Ended Questions That Replace "Why" Questions
Why did you ask him into your apartment?	How did things get out of control in your apartment?
Why did you smoke crack?	What was it like to decide to smoke crack?
Why did you try to kill yourself?	What was going through your mind when you took the pills?
How do these questions make you feel?	

Clarifying

Clarification questions are a form of soft closed-ended questions. Counselors use this basic attending skill when they aren't quite sure of what the client just said. Maybe they missed a piece of information because the client was speaking too fast, or presented so much information at once that the crisis worker just couldn't grasp it all. In clarifying, counselors restate in their own words what they thought they heard clients say in a questioning manner, beginning the statement with "are you saying," or "did you mean". The clarifying technique is used to clear up confusion or ambiguity and thus avoid misunderstanding and confirm the accuracy of what counselors heard. Clients might then be asked to rephrase or restate a previous message. The question is not meant to encourage clients to explore more of what was said, but simply to help counselors make sure that they understood what was said. Sometimes, clients talk in such a fragmented manner or so rapidly that important facts and ideas may not be heard accurately, and clarifying aids counselors in clearly understanding what was said.

> **Box 4.2   Paraphrasing and Clarifying Exercise**
>
> Choose a partner, and ask a third person to be an observer. One person plays the crisis interviewer, and one plays a client in crisis. After the client tells the counselor about the crisis, the counselor is to restate in her own words what was heard. Do not parrot or repeat exactly what was said. Sometimes it is helpful for the counselor to break out of character and tell the observer, in the third person, what she heard the client say. The counselor can then go back into character and talk directly to the client, paraphrasing what she heard the client say. The dialogue shows how this might work:
>
> CLIENT: "I've been depressed since I had to have my dog put to sleep last week. I can't sleep or concentrate at work and everyone thinks I'm a big baby."
>
> CRISIS WORKER: "Are you saying that you have felt very bad since your dog died and aren't receiving any support from your coworkers?" (Clarifying)
>
> CRISIS WORKER: "I hear you saying that since putting your dog to sleep last week, you've been unable to sleep and feel depressed, and no one at work seems to understand your feelings." (Restatement)

Paraphrasing

Paraphrasing is when counselors restate in their own words what they thought they heard clients say. The crisis worker does not seek to parrot or simply repeat exactly what the client said, but instead the goal is to share with the client what was heard by the counselor. The focus is on the cognitive and factual part of the client's message. The intent is to encourage elaboration of the statements to let the client know that you, the counselor, have understood or heard the message; to help the client focus on a specific situation, idea, or action; and to highlight content when attention to affect would be premature or inappropriate (Slaikeu, 1990, p. 38). Try the paraphrase/clarification exercise provided in Box 4.2.

Reflection of Feelings

Empathy is integral to achieving and maintaining contact with clients. This means being able to let clients know you understand their feelings. The technique of **reflection**, which is a statement that reflects the affective part or emotional tone of the client's message, whether verbal or nonverbal, is a powerful tool in creating an empathic environment. Not only does it help clarify the client's feelings in a particular situation, but it also helps the client feel understood. Clients can then express their own feelings about a situation; learn to manage their feelings, especially negative ones; and express their feelings toward the mental health care provider and agency. As we saw in Chapter 1, Caplan proposed that one characteristic of people who are coping effectively

---

Box 4.3   Reflection of Feelings Exercise

In pairs or in a group, have someone role-play a client in crisis, who will tell the others of his or her problem and feelings. Each student counselor then restates just the feelings to the client. Listen to the emotional tone and look for nonverbal cues, such as eyes watering or a fist pounding. Try using these openings: "You seem to feel...," "Sounds as though you feel...," "I sense you are...." Look for ambivalent and contradictory feelings as well as positive feelings.

Here are some examples:

Painful feelings: "Sounds like you are furious with your wife."
Positive feelings: "You seem to be happiest when you don't drink."
Ambivalent feelings: "Although you say you hate your husband, you also seem to pity him."
Nonverbal feelings: "I can see by the tears in your eyes how painful this loss is."

---

is their ability to express feelings freely and master them. Reflection of feelings allows such a process to occur.

Therapists from Freud to Rogers have believed that catharsis and experiential awareness of feelings are the curative factors in therapy. The crisis interview might be the only time the client has ever felt validated in her or his feelings, and that is usually a good experience in and of itself! Try the reflection exercise presented in Box 4.3.

Summarization

The key purpose of **summarization** is to help another individual pull his or her thoughts together. A secondary purpose is to check on whether you as a helper have distorted the client's frame of reference. Summarization may be helpful in beginning an interview if you've seen the client previously; it may help to bring together threads of data over several interviews or simply clarify what has gone on in the present interview (Ivey et al., 1997, p. 92). This is an example of a summarization: "So, your husband beat you last night and this time hit your daughter. You are scared and lonely and don't know where to turn."

As will be discussed in the "B" section below, summarization can help make a smooth transition from identifying the problem to finding coping strategies. Usually, the cognitive and affective content are restated as well as the precipitating event and coping efforts. These aspects are easy to remember if you keep in mind the three aspects of any crisis: (1) the precipitating event; (2) the perception of the event by the client, which leads to subjective distress; and (3) the failure of the client to cope successfully with the distress.

Now that you've learned the basic attending skills, practice them in 7- to 10-minute role-plays using the evaluation sheet in Table 4.1. Once you have mastered these skills, you are ready to move on to more advanced communication skills. The basic attending skills will be used throughout every session.

They help counselors maintain rapport and allow them access to delicate information about the client. Counselors will use these basic attending skills during both the "B" and "C" stages of the ABC model. Notice how the ABC model is presented as three stages, but that "A" covers both "B" and "C".

B: Identifying the Problem

After demographic information has been gathered and as rapport is developing, the crisis worker starts to focus on the client's presenting crisis. Identifying the problem is the second step in the ABC method and is the most crucial one. Refer to the ABC model of crisis intervention outline in Table 4.2 for a look at the interview process. Each aspect is examined individually as well as in the context of the others in the process. The most effective counselors become so well-versed in the various aspects of this model that they do not appear mechanical to the client. Keeping in mind the definition of crisis helps counselors remember what to identify: precipitating events, perceptions, subjective distress, and functioning.

Although the model is presented in a linear outline form, interviews do not have to be conducted in a linear fashion. Unfortunately for beginning counselors, having a script for each crisis situation is just not practical. However, the examples presented can be used in conjunction with the counselors' creative processes and intuition. This outline will be useful for you as you practice each type of crisis in subsequent chapters. In each of those chapters, examples are given for practice in role-playing. Do not be restricted to using only the ideas given. Create your own ideas whenever possible. The outline can be used for a 10-minute phone call, a 50-minute session, or a 6-week (or longer) series of crisis intervention sessions. Each week, new issues can be addressed and new coping strategies sought while changes in functioning can be assessed from week to week. Notice that the model has several areas to assess. This does not mean that on every visit the counselor must make an assessment for each area. Rather, each area should be addressed at least on the first or second visit and then reassessed thereafter as necessary to evaluate the client's progress.

Of particular importance in crisis intervention and in brief therapy is the ability to explore the client's perceptions. Most sessions will be spent in this process, and through these explorations clients gain knowledge of the source of their pain. Once clients' perceptions and frame of reference regarding various situations are understood, the crisis worker is in a position to guide clients into new ways of thinking and experiencing themselves and the world. Also, once clients' cognitions are changed, subjective distress will be reduced, coping skills can be implemented, and functioning will be increased. This, as you will recall, is the goal of crisis intervention (review the beginning of chapter one).

The interview process can be thought of as climbing a tree with the client (see Figure 4.2). The client will usually present with the precipitating event or subjective distress such as emotional pain or impairment in functioning. The goal of the B section is to "climb the tree" to explore how all the components are related to the cognitions.

TABLE 4.2   ABC Model of Crisis Intervention

A: Use of Basic Attending Skills to Develop and Maintain Rapport

Attending behaviors
Opening-ended questions
Paraphrasing
Reflection of feelings
Clarifying
Close-ended questions
Reflection of feelings
Clarifying
Close-ended questions Summarizations

B: Identifying the Nature of the Crisis and Therapeutic Interaction

Identify the precipitating event
Identify cognitions
Identify subjective distress
Identify impairments in functioning:
Behaviorally, socially, academically, occupationally
Ethical checks:
Suicide, homicide, organic issues, psychosis, substance abuse, child abuse, elder abuse
Therapeutic interaction statements:
Educational, empowerment, validation, reframes

C: Coping Strategies

Explore what client wants to do now to cope
Explore what client has tried in the past to cope
Explore other things client can do to cope
Offer alternative strategies for coping:
Support groups
Twelve-step groups
Marital or family therapy
Lawyer
Doctor
Bibliotherapy
Reel therapy
Assertion training
Stress management
Shelters or other agencies
Secure commitment and follow-up

The counselor climbs up the trunk with the client by asking what the client's thoughts are about the trunk. These thoughts are explored by asking the client to further explain what the client means. Open-ended questions are used to help the client explore all related thoughts and perceptions until the leaves are understood—they are the cognitive key. The counselor can help change the leaves from brown to green with therapeutic interaction comments.

FIGURE 4.2 The Cognition
Tree

Cognition 1 Is a Branch
[Twigs and leaves explore this
cognition—leaves are brown
(cognitive key)]

Cognition 2 Is a Branch
[Twigs and leaves explore this
cognition—leaves are brown
(cognitive key)]

Cognition 3 Is a Branch
[Twigs and leaves explore this
cognition—leaves are brown
(cognitive key)]

Clients present a trunk: a
precipitating event, emotions, or
impairments in functioning

Examples of therapeutic interaction comments can be found in many sections
of subsequent chapters and will be defined clearly later in this chapter. Many
times, several important cognitions are presented. Each one will have to be
explored and new therapeutic comments then provided. Identifying cognitions
and offering new ways of thinking about the situation is the main focus of
crisis intervention sessions using the ABC Model.

By exploring the many limbs and twigs of the initial perception presented,
the counselor and client gain a deeper understanding of what is really bothering the client most about the precipitating event. It often takes as many as six
questions before the cognitive key can be established and therapeutic statements offered. If the counselor attempts to provide an educational statement,
a reframe, a **support statement**, or an empowerment statement too soon, the
client often resists. The client probably just needed more time to fully explain
his or her cognitive tree. Below is a sample dialogue in which therapist and
client climb the tree:

CLIEN: "My husband left me." (Presents a precipitating event)

COUNSELOR: "What does that mean to you?" (Asks open-ended question to
explore perception)

CLIENT: "I will be alone forever." (First cognition presented; client thinks she'll
be alone forever)

COUNSELOR: "In what way alone?" (Counselor tries to understand exactly
what client means by "alone")

CLIENT: "No one will ever love me again." (New cognitive statement)

COUNSELOR: "What makes you think that?"

CLIENT: "He told me that he's the only one who could ever love me because I'm so ugly and stupid." (More new information about the original cognition)

COUNSELOR: "What are your thoughts about the idea of your being ugly and stupid?"

CLIENT: "Well, I don't think I'm really that stupid."

COUNSELOR: "What do you think?'

CLIENT: "I'm afraid to be alone and start all over."

COUNSELOR: "What is most scary for you about this?"

CLIENT: "I'm afraid to get close to someone else and feel hurt."

COUNSELOR: "It is often scary to start over." (Support statement that validates client's feelings and thoughts) "This scary feeling may at some point turn into excitement at the opportunity to have a more rewarding relationship." (A brief reframe of the scariness possibly being excitement)

At this point, the client may feel some hope and her cognitions will probably have changed to some extent. Notice how many questions were necessary to reach the deeper meanings behind her initial cognition.

Probably the most important reason for exploring the client's internal frame of reference is that changing internal perceptions is easier than changing external situations. If the crisis worker spends too much time focusing on the significant others and the details of the situation—elements that generally cannot be changed—the client may experience increased frustration.

At the end of this chapter, a "script" using the ABC model of crisis intervention is presented. It offers specific questions and statements a crisis worker might use. It is presented after readers have had a chance to learn about each section of the model individually. Then they should be able to understand how to integrate all the sections in a typical interview.

Identifying the Precipitating Event

Shortly after the interview begins, the counselor seeks to find out about the precipitating event. To ask, "What happened that made you call for an appointment?" is appropriate. It is an opening for clients to tell what is going on with them. If clients cannot think of any particular event that brought them to counseling, the crisis worker is encouraged to probe further, explaining that understanding the trigger of a client's crisis aids in relieving the crisis state.

The precipitating event may have happened yesterday or six weeks ago. A helpful strategy is learning when the client started to feel bad, which helps pinpoint the triggering event. "The straw that broke the camel's back" is a common expression that can help clients focus on the beginning of the crisis.

Another reason for specifying the precipitating event is to be able, later on, to explore how the client has been trying to cope since it happened. When the client's denial is strong, the crisis worker can confront the client about why exactly the client decided to come for counseling. The reason is usually because of difficulty in coping with a precipitating event. If the event is not clearly defined, the counselor will have problems presenting alternative coping strategies to deal with the event. Last, identification of the precipitating event is vital because the crisis worker must identify the client's perceptions about the episode. If these cognitions are not identified properly, there can be no therapeutic interactive comments related to them. Remember, change in the way the event is perceived is essential to increasing the functioning level of clients. In Chapter 1, two formulas were presented and are repeated here. Refer to them as you practice using the ABC model.

FIGURE 4.3   Formula for Understanding the Process of Crisis Formation

Precipitating Event   ⟶   Perception   ⟶   Subjective Distress   ⟶   Lowered Functioning (When Coping Fails)

FIGURE 4.4   Formula to Increase Functioning

Change in Perception of the Precipitating Event and Acquiring New Coping Skills   ⟶   Decrease in Subjective Distress   ⟶   Increase in Functioning

If the goal of crisis work is to increase clients' functioning, the following formula aids crisis workers in understanding how to move clients out of a crisis.

No matter how much clients profess that "nothing has happened, really," something drove them to seek help. Squeeze it out of them! They need to see that their current state of subjective distress is tied to an actual event or fact.

Recognizing the Meaning or Perception of the Precipitating Event

In addition to identifying precipitating events, crisis workers actively explore the meaning clients ascribe to these events. It is clients' perceptions of stressful situations that cause them to be in a crisis state as well as the inability to cope with the stress. Usually, stress originates from one of four areas: loss of control, loss of self-esteem, loss of nurturance, or forced adjustment to a change in life or role. The meaning behind these losses is helpful to explore.

All aspects of the situation will be examined. For example, suppose a woman is raped. Not only does the actual rape cause stress, but her perception of how her husband will react also contributes to her stress as she struggles with her perceived new role with him.

Some questions the crisis worker may ask to elicit the client's frame of reference regarding the crisis situation include these:

- "How do you put it together in your head?"
- "What do you think about this?"
- "What does it mean to you that...?"
- "What are you telling yourself about...?"
- "What assumptions are you making about...?"

Cognitive restructuring or reframing is a valuable tool for the counselor but can be done only if the client's current cognitions are known. It is impossible to develop a coping plan for clients without examining the cognitive and perceptual experience. Think of yourself as a mechanic who needs to analyze and experience the trouble firsthand before tinkering with the engine. Crisis workers can think of themselves as "cognitive mechanics."

Assessing the client's perception of the precipitating event is one of the most important parts of the interview and is to be done thoroughly on every visit to check for changing views as well as long-standing views on a variety of issues.

Identifying Subjective Distress and Functioning Level

In addition to exploring stressors and clients' perceptions of them, counselors also inquire about clients' functioning and how the precipitating events are affecting it. Clients seem to benefit from expressing painful feelings and sharing other symptoms—symptoms that may impair clients' occupational, academic, behavioral, social, interpersonal, or family functioning. Counselors can ask how clients' perceptions about the precipitating event are affecting their functioning in each area.

Often each area in which the person is suffering distress is dealt with separately because a specific perception may be associated with that area and not another. The crisis worker is advised to explore each area affected during the crisis state in as much detail as possible. This probing gives the counselor a feel for the degree of impairment the client is experiencing and can be used later to help select coping strategies. When clients discuss their symptoms and impairments in functioning, they can receive feedback, education, and support from the counselor. Often, understanding one's feelings and behaviors is the first step in coping with them. Box 4.4 below gives some examples that might help you understand the importance of a thorough assessment of functioning.

Most intake forms ask for a comparison between current and previous functioning on a regular basis. It is important to include this information as part of any crisis assessment procedure.

Making Ethical Checks

Several other areas are usually identified in an initial interview. These have ethical implications and are assessed either directly or indirectly with every client. However, in order not to behave like a prosecuting attorney, the crisis worker is encouraged to extract this information in a fluid, relevant manner.

> **Box 4.4**
>
> **Example 1:** A battered woman might be experiencing much anxiety at work because she believes that her husband will come there and cause a scene, which would probably result in her being fired. This perception might be dealt with by letting her know that bosses can often be sympathetic and helpful, and that her boss might even provide her with support and initiate legal action for her.
>
> In addition to identifying the client's current level of functioning, the crisis worker may wish to assess the client's precrisis level of functioning in order to compare the two. This will help the counselor determine the level of coping the client can realistically achieve; it also gives the counselor an idea of the severity of the crisis for the person. The comparison serves as a basis for evaluating the outcome of crisis intervention. Remember that the goal of crisis intervention is to bring the client back to the precrisis level of functioning.
>
> **Example 2:** If a woman was getting straight As in college before being raped, and afterward her grades went down to Cs and Ds, her crisis was worse for her than for a woman who was raped but showed only minimal disturbance at work or school. In these cases, it is probable that the first woman's perception of the rape was more drastic than the second woman's. Maybe she told herself that she was at fault, that she is dirty, and that no one will ever love her again. The second woman might have a more realistic view of the rape and be able to tell herself that it was the rapist's fault, and that no one is going to hold her responsible or think differently about her.

Rather than going down a list and asking one question after another, the skillful counselor weaves the questions in as the issues arise in the normal flow of the conversation.

Suicide Check   Because people in crisis are vulnerable and often confused and overwhelmed, suicide sometimes becomes an alternative for them. Every crisis worker must assess for suicidality, particularly when the client is depressed or impulsive. Suicide assessment and prevention are discussed in detail in Chapter 5.

Homicidal/Abuse Issues   As discussed in the ethics chapter, mental health workers in many states are required to report child and elder abuse and any suspicion that a client may harm someone. Assessment of these issues must be done during the course of an interview. Often, the counselor's intuition will provide the basis for detailed inquiry. Child abuse and elder abuse are dealt with in subsequent chapters; working with clients who are a danger to others is examined in Chapter 5. Two examples of appropriate ethical checks are provided below in Box 4.5.

Making clients part of the reporting process helped them deal with it in a less fearful manner. The counselor had no choice but to make the report, even though the clients did not want her to.

Organic or Other Concerns   If clients state that they suffer from serious **depression, bipolar disorder,** obsessive-compulsive disorder, or **schizophrenia,** they should already be receiving medication. Crisis workers can assess for medication compliance for these cases and encourage noncompliant clients to

---

Box 4.5   Examples of Homicidal/Abuse Issues

Example 1: A 43-year-old male may say that he hates his father for having beaten his mother and can see himself smashing the father's face. This statement alone does not warrant an attempt to take the client into custody. However, I would inquire how he deals with this anger, especially toward his wife and children. It is important for counselors to know that suspected abuse of children must be assessed in all cases. Sometimes, turning away and collaborating in denial with an abusive family is easier than facing the issue, but doing so is never in the best interest of the child. Such action is unethical and might be illegal, depending on the laws of the state where the action occurs.

Example 2: The mother of a 15-year-old boy and a 16-year-old girl is in a crisis state and seeks help from a counselor. Two weeks earlier, the husband whipped the boy with a belt and left welts on his back. The father also slapped the girl across the face. When the mother was informed by the crisis worker that a child abuse report would have to be made, she was very upset and pleaded with the therapist not to make the report. She thought that it would affect her getting a high-security job for which she was applying; would make the husband angry; and would cause anxiety for her son, who was worried that his dad would take his car away. The counselor explained that a report was mandatory in this situation. To alleviate the mother's concern, the counselor made the report in the presence of the clients, so they would know what would most likely happen according to the social worker taking the call.

---

continue with prescribed medication until they can schedule an appointment with their physician. In these situations, crisis workers may want to consult with the physician by phone to ensure that clients receive the most effective treatment. When clients describe or exhibit behaviors, symptoms, or complaints that may be due to biological factors such as Alzheimer's disease or attention deficit disorder with hyperactivity (ADHD) or any other **organic brain disorder** but have not yet been formally diagnosed with a serious disorder, ethical standards require crisis workers to refer them to a physician or psychiatrist for further assessment. Chapter 5 presents a brief discussion of how to use the Mental Status Exam to assess for these serious medical disorders.

Substance Abuse Issues

Checking for substance abuse on a regular basis is a good idea and is often part of the intake form in most agencies. Because clients involved with substance use and abuse often deny and minimize their use, the crisis worker might be a bit more assertive in gathering information about drug use. Following are some examples showing how to extract this information without offending clients:

> *"Tell me about your past and present drug and alcohol use."*

> *This statement assumes that use exists or existed and is stated matter-of-factly, as if you won't be shocked to hear of it. The person who has not used drugs can simply say "None."*

> *"How much alcohol do you use a week?"*

"What other drugs besides cocaine do you use or have you used?"

These questions do not seem to be as judgmental or grilling as the following do:

"Do you use alcohol? Do you use cocaine? Do you smoke pot? Do you drink daily?"

Using general, open-ended questions will save time and reduce defensiveness in clients.

Therapeutic Interaction

The main part of the session, and probably the most therapeutic part, will be spent in identifying the client's beliefs and feelings, and then providing supportive statements, educational information, **empowering statements**, and reframing statements that will aid the client in thinking differently about the situation and assist them in coping with it. Of course, active listening skills remain important, but once these are used to identify the nature of the crisis, the counselor is ready to use the more advanced skills discussed next to help clients improve their coping ability.

Validation and Support Statements   The counselor may, from time to time, tell clients that their feelings are normal or suggest there is hope that things will get better. In response to a woman who has just found out that her husband has been molesting their daughter and feels as though the world has come to an end, a crisis worker might respond supportively by saying, "I know that right now you feel that everything is falling apart, but many people have gone through the same situation and have survived. You have every reason to believe you can survive, too." Other validation comments that are useful include, "It is understandable that you might feel that way," "Your pain is understandable considering how difficult your situation is," or "Many people going through this would also feel and think this way."

Support statements are not false hopes or words like "It'll be okay," "Don't worry," or "Forget about it." These comments are typical of family and friends who mean well; however, they are not very useful. As crisis workers, we need to say things to people that others do not say. Also, because clients see counselors as experts in crisis situations, they will tend to take comfort in supportive comments from these helpers, often adopting a more optimistic attitude. Receiving validation from a counselor about one's feelings can help clients not see themselves as sick, weak, or bad.

Educational Statements   Providing factual information, whether developmental or situational, is vital in every crisis. Clients often suffer merely because they lack or have incorrect knowledge about the precipitating event and aspects associated with it. Thus, it is imperative for crisis workers to gather as much information as possible about each crisis situation. Whether this is done through formal academic courses, books, experience, or supervision, it gives counselors an edge in helping clients work through their issues. General knowledge of statistics and prevelance rates of various traumas that often trigger crises states are vital for effective crisis intervention.

Educational statements may include psychological, social, and interpersonal dynamics, or they may provide statistics or frequency of the problem. In any case, when a counselor helps people in a crisis state increase their knowledge of facts, the clients will have stronger coping skills for the current crisis and future crises. You will remember from Chapter 1 that seeking reality and information was one of Caplan's characteristics of effective coping behavior. Box 4.6 gives an example of the use of an educational statement.

Box 4.6   Example of the Use of an Educational Statement

Picture a woman who has been completely isolated from others because she is in an ongoing battering relationship. She will most likely perceive herself as abnormal and bizarre. When she learns that about 30 percent of women live in such relationships, she may feel differently about herself and the abnormality of the situation. Without this issue to deal with, the counselor is now free to process other issues.

Empowering Statements   Clients who are in certain crisis situations in which they feel violated, victimized, or helpless respond well to **empowering statements**. Clients are presented with choices and are encouraged to take back personal power by making helpful choices. Battered women, rape survivors, and survivors of child abuse often suffer from learned helplessness stemming from the abuse. They think that they cannot prevent bad things from happening because, in the past, they could not prevent abuse by a physically stronger (or in some other way stronger) perpetrator. This perception often motivates them to survive abuse rather than try and escape from it. A useful strategy is to let clients know that they may not have had the choice to stop the abuse from happening at an earlier time but that now they certainly can make choices to do something about the abuse (e.g., press charges, confront the perpetrator, talk about it). Also, the crisis worker can point out that they do not have to choose certain behaviors. It is important that they move from a position of feeling powerless to feeling that they have some control and choice in their life now. See Box 4.7 for an example of an empowerment statement.

Box 4.7   Example of the Use of an Empowerment Statement

Example: A rape victim might be told, "You didn't have a choice in being raped, but now you do have a choice of what to do. You can call the police, go to counseling, tell a friend, or not do any of these things. Let's talk about your feelings and thoughts on each of these choices."

Reframing Statements   In its simplest form, **reframing** is defining a situation differently from the way the client is defining it. It is a cognitive restructuring tactic that aims at changing the crisis from danger to opportunity. American clichés such as, "Every cloud has a silver lining" and "When life gives you lemons, make lemonade" convey this idea quite clearly.

Reframing may seem like rationalizing away a problem to some. However, it is probably one of the strongest healing skills available to the crisis worker and for people in general. It allows us to acknowledge that life is a struggle, that we aren't perfect, and that dwelling on our failings is not necessary or helpful. Instead, if we can believe that something positive or beneficial will be an outcome or result of the problem, we can usually integrate the difficult episode more easily. The crisis worker's responsibility is to be creative in finding the right reframe, which means actively searching for the positive. Reframing is an advanced technique that puts problems in a solvable form by changing the meanings of behaviors and situations and providing a new perspective that opens up new possibilities for change. Box 4.8 below shows an example of reframing.

Box 4.8

Example: The author worked with a woman whose rape case was rejected by the district attorney after she had hoped for a year that it would go to court. The rapist was free, and her victimization had not been acknowledged because of a legal technicality. The counselor and client could have both thrown up their hands, called the judicial system names, and seethed internally. Alternatively, the counselor pointed out to the client that the rape prodded her to seek counseling that allowed her not only to work through the rape issues, but also to identify her codependency and its effects on her relationships. This knowledge led the way to better family relations and intimacy with her boyfriend. The reframe was that the rape, although terrifying, had been survived and indirectly allowed for an opportunity to gain self-understanding and growth. This client could tolerate this reframe because she had undergone one year of intensive therapy and had strong rapport with the counselor, who truly understood the client's frame of reference.

Reframing is possible only if the counselor first understands fully the client's current frame of reference. Otherwise, the counselor would not know what should be reframed. Counselors can learn the client's frame of reference by asking direct questions: "How do you perceive the situation?" "What does it mean to you?" "What runs through your head about it?" Reframing is not a technique to be taken lightly, and careful supervision is necessary in learning its effective use. Sometimes reframing is associated with a cold, strategic approach, but it can be done in an authentic, caring manner. The counselor does not deny the seriousness of the problem but instead offers a way out of a problem that allows the person to preserve the integrity of the self and often the family unit as well. Because reframes are usually offered with the person's self-identity in mind, shame is reduced and self-integrity is preserved. Because reframing is challenging for beginning counselors, examples of potential reframes are provided in subsequent chapters. It may take severalyears for a counselor to learn the art of reframing. Brainstorming with others is a useful way to learn how to formulate reframes.

In summary, the B section of the ABC model can be thought of as identifying issues one at a time and providing various forms of feedback as the process moves forward to a place where the client can accept coping as viable behavior. Periodically, the crisis worker summarizes the precipitating events, the client's perceptions of them, the client's functioning in several areas of life, and any major symptoms of concern.

C: Coping

The last step of the ABC model is concerned with the client's coping behavior—past, present, and future. Past coping success can be built on to help the person weather the present and future difficulties.

Exploring the Client's Own Attempts at Coping

Toward the conclusion of an interview, counselors begin summing up the problem and moving clients into a coping mode. To do this, crisis workers ask clients what they would like to do now to start coping with the problem. If clients cannot think of anything, they might be asked how they have managed crises in the past. All coping, whether it is helpful or not, should be examined. In this way, clients can make a mental list of what works and what does not.

If clients cannot think of any past coping behavior, the crisis worker can assertively encourage them. The counselor might say, "Well, you must have done something or you would not have made it this far." Remember that even sleeping and social withdrawal are coping strategies, and the counselor and client can talk about their helpfulness or unhelpfulness. Eliciting unhealthy attempts at coping is especially valuable as it helps the client see what has not worked in the past. The client will generally be more open to alternatives once the ineffectiveness of his or her current behavior is made evident.

Encouraging the Development of New Coping Behaviors

After current ideas about what the client might like to do now to cope and current and past coping attempts have been discussed, the counselor can prod clients to ponder other possible ways of coping. Remember that clients have already been presented with educational information, reframes, supportive comments, and empowerment statements. It is time for clients to do some of their own thinking. Clients are more likely to follow through with a plan they have developed themselves than with one suggested by the counselor. It is appropriate for a counselor to be challenging and persistent in getting clients to think of ways they could begin to cope better. This approach helps clients get in touch with their problem-solving abilities.

Presenting Alternative Coping Behaviors

Clients are first allowed to propose their own methods for coping with their problems. When they have reached the end of the resources they know, however, the counselor can then suggest other options. Many of these may be completely new to clients, offering them fresh insights. The suggestions offered by the counselor are best based on previous discussions with the client. The client will often provide the counselor with the best alternative for that particular client. For example, a client might have said that one of the things that made her feel better was talking to her girlfriends about her divorce. But now, she says, they are tired of listening. This might trigger in the counselor the idea that this client feels better talking to a group of women about her problem. Getting the client to accept a referral to a support group should not be difficult, because the client herself has said that doing this type of thing has already made her feel better!

Support Groups and Twelve-Step Groups   If support systems haven't already been discussed, now is a good time to identify some existing natural support, such as coworkers, supervisors, relatives, friends, schoolmates, or church members. Clients may not have considered any of these people as helpers in getting through the crisis. With a little encouragement, they may be persuaded to reach out to others. This is not to suggest that crisis workers should avoid giving support to clients. However, it is often more comfortable for clients to receive help from natural **support systems** than to rely on mental health professionals during crises. As Caplan (1964) suggested earlier, people who are coping effectively with a situation will actively ask others for help, not necessarily mental health workers. The idea of encouraging clients to help themselves parallels the adage of teaching a man to fish versus just giving him fish. Self-sufficiency is more economical in the long run. The author has often felt that as a crisis interventionist, her job is to put herself out of a job by encouraging clients to function on their own and with the support of others in their life. A crisis worker is merely a beacon shedding light on these resources.

Some clients may need referrals to twelve-step groups such as Alcoholics Anonymous (AA), Al-Anon, Co-Dependents Anonymous, Cocaine Anonymous, or others. These mutual self-help groups are free and have no time limits for attendance; sessions can be found in every city at various hours of the day. The trend now is for insurance companies to pay for only six to 12 sessions of therapy, so twelve-step groups are a lifesaver for many people who cannot afford to pay for therapy out of their own pockets.

Long-Term Therapy, Marital Therapy, and Family Therapy   Some clients' problems have been going on for so long that crisis intervention cannot resolve them. Perhaps because of a personality disorder or other chronic emotional disorder, clients need ongoing therapy with a trained professional. This might be individual therapy or marital or family therapy. Often, a crisis is an opportunity for clients to resolve long-term problems that have been hidden for many years.

Shelters and Other Agencies   To address other problems, crisis workers need to be knowledgeable about community agencies and **resources**. Clients who are anxious and feeling overwhelmed are more likely to follow through with a referral when it is presented in written form with choices, addresses, phone numbers, and fees. Providing written information is much more effective than telling clients to look for certain services in the Yellow Pages. Even if you are conducting a phone interview, having these resources in hand, separated by the type of crisis, certainly aids the expediency of referral. Also, crisis workers will know whether an agency can actually help a client at an affordable rate if workers have recently updated their information about the agency.

Most communities have community resource directories that list various agencies, and local libraries also have listings available. One of the best ways to get names of agencies is by contacting an agency that has similar services. Most mental health and social service agencies are familiar with agencies in the community.

A useful assignment for beginning crisis intervention students is to do research on various community agencies and resources that regularly intervene in crisis situations. It is amazing to learn how many resources are available in most communities for almost any crisis situation. Community resources were developed during the grassroots era of the 1960s, and they have evolved over the years into an elaborate networking system of many different agencies. Large organizations often have nationwide toll-free phone numbers that workers can call to get information about many agencies. The organizations serve as clearinghouses for a variety of resources. Some examples of community resources include local churches, local community colleges, county mental health agencies, local AA groups, and private clubs such as the Sierra Club.

Some resources are more appropriate for certain crises than others. Suicidal clients should be given a list of hotlines to call, if necessary, between sessions. Persons suffering a loss from divorce might be referred to a divorce recovery workshop through a church or support group. Clients dealing with issues related to HIV or AIDS should be referred to a local AIDS services foundation for support groups. It is widely known that substance abusers and their significant others benefit from twelve-step groups such as AA or Al-Anon. Sexual assault victims and battered women benefit from a referral to shelters or specialized support groups.

At times, crisis workers may want to contact an agency and let someone there know about a referral. It is quite reasonable to ask for a follow-up call or note about whether the client used the resource. In other instances, a client may return to a crisis worker for another individual session and the crisis worker at that time can ask whether the client attended the support group or used the service recommended.

Medical and Legal Referrals   In some cases, **medical or legal referrals** are necessary. Even crisis workers who are considered paraprofessionals should have an understanding of the legal, political, and medical systems and how they will make an impact on various types of crises. For instance, workers should know the conditions under which a police officer may arrest a battering spouse. Also, they should have knowledge of restraining orders, which may be useful for a victim of abuse. How the court system generally deals with rape or child abuse is useful information as well. Though they are not expected to be lawyers, crisis workers need to keep abreast of recent laws that affect clients in crisis.

Similarly, though they are not expected or allowed to be physicians, crisis workers need to be able to refer someone to a doctor for an evaluation when medication or other treatment might be useful. Learning to consult and work with medical doctors is a skill worth developing, and knowing when to make a referral to a physician is vital.

Bibliotherapy, Journaling, and Reel Therapy   It would be optimal for every crisis worker to have some knowledge of reading material for clients in a variety of crisis situations. Using these materials with clients is called **bibliotherapy**. Reading often provides a new way of looking at the crisis (reframing) and gives the client information and support—especially books written by a person who has gone through a similar crisis. For example, reading a book by a woman who was raped will help the recently raped woman see that her feelings are normal; this knowledge should have a calming effect. Also, reading helps people think rather than feel, encouraging more productive problem-solving activity. Having clients keep a journal of their thoughts is also quite helpful; the clients may discover new feelings and thoughts as they jot them down on paper. The journal may be shared with the counselor or remain private.

Many therapists are also using movies to help move their clients toward breakthroughs more quickly. Viewing movies allows clients to "grow" in their own "free" time. For example, Nielsen (quoted in Hesley, 2000, pp. 55–57) has used the movie *Distant Thunder* for clients experiencing posttraumatic stress disorder. He states that many of his clients find it easier to explain their own "flashbacks" and "social phobia" after viewing this film. The use of films—so-called **reel therapy**—is likely to become more common because many future therapists watch films as part of their graduate school studies. Films do have limitations and should not take the place of personal discussion with the counselor. Movies should be selected carefully and thoughtfully (Hesley, 2000, pp. 55–57).

Other Behavioral Activities   Some clients may benefit from assertiveness training, in which the counselor teaches them how to ask for what they want, express feelings and needs to others, or set boundaries with others. Other tasks may include having clients exercise, visit friends and family, or engage in a recreational activity such as going to the beach. Stress management classes may also be useful for helping clients organize their time and daily life activities.

All of these types of coping referrals provide ways for the client to cope and think differently about the precipitating event.

Commitment and Follow-Up

Part of making any referral or suggestion is **commitment and follow-up**; that is, counselors get a commitment from clients that they will indeed follow through with recommendations. This explains why it is best for clients to develop their own coping plans; they are more likely to follow through with a plan they have formulated themselves. In some cases, as with highly suicidal clients, a written contract may be prudent. The no-suicide contract is a useful intervention that will be discussed in Chapter five. Written contracts are often used with clients who need to control their impulses or with acting-out teenagers. Both the therapist and the client keep a copy of the contract and discuss it at the next session.

In sum, the C part of the ABC model first asks clients to explore current, past, and possibly new coping strategies to deal with the crisis at hand. Then the crisis worker offers alternative ideas, makes referrals, and asks clients for a commitment to follow through on the plan. The worker's hope is that clients will move from a dysfunctional state to a higher level of functioning and perceived control over the precipitating event. At each visit, the crisis worker can verify and suggest connecting with these various coping aids, which gives clients something concrete to take home.

Chapter Review

The ABC model of crisis intervention is a structured short-term approach to help people work through a variety of situational and developmental crises. It is based loosely on Jones's ABC crisis management model, Adler's four-stage model of therapy, and on the current needs of non-profit agencies, HMO centers, and public mental health agencies. The A section refers to the use of basic attending skills to develop and maintain rapport while identifying the information in the B and C sections. Attending behavior, paraphrasing, clarifying, reflection, open-ended questions, and summarizations are the crux of these basic attending skills. During the B section, the nature of the crisis is identified, and therapeutic comments are presented by the counselor. After identifying the precipitating event, the cognitions associated with the event, the subjective distress, and impairments in functioning, the crisis worker is able to provide feedback such as reframes, empowerment statements, educational statements, and validation statements. In the C section, coping strategies are developed by the client and counselor together.

Correct Answers to Pre-Chapter Quiz

1. T   2. F   3. F   4. T   5. T   6. T   7. F   8. F   9. T   10. F

Key Terms for Study

attending behavior: Behavior that has to do with following the client's lead, actively listening, and demonstrating presence.

bibliotherapy: The use of books as an alternative coping strategy.

bipolar disorder: A condition in which states of manic behavior (i.e., out-of-control, hyper, grandiose behavior) fluctuate with states of extreme depression. It is sometimes known as manic-depression.

close-ended question: A type of question that can be answered with a "yes" or a "no" or some other one-word answer. Its best use is for obtaining facts such as age, number of children, or number of years married. Forced-choice questions, or "do you, have you" questions, are generally not effective. These types of questions can bring the interview to a dead end or sound like an interrogation.

commitment and follow-up: Verbal agreement given by client to a crisis worker at the end of a crisis intervention session. Specifically, it is what the client is going to do after leaving the session to deal with the crisis. It may include returning to see the same counselor or going elsewhere. Remember that the person in crisis is vulnerable and needs direction.

depression: A state of being in which the client is sad, low in energy, and suicidal; he or she feels worthless, helpless, and hopeless; the person lacks desire, is socially withdrawn, and is slowed in processes such as thinking and concentrating. This person should be referred to a physician for an evaluation.

educational statements: Types of therapeutic comments in which facts, statistics, and theories are presented to clients in an attempt to normalize their experience and change their misconceptions.

empowering statements: Therapeutic comments that help clients feel more in control and see choices they have. They are especially useful for clients who have been victimized.

medical or legal referrals: Referrals made by the crisis worker if the client needs the services of other professionals, as when a person has been arrested, wants a restraining order, or has a severe mental or other illness.

open-ended questions: The questions ususally begin with "what" and "how" and allow clients to expand on material they have brought up on their own.

organic brain disorder: A condition resulting from a neurological disturbance, genetic abnormality, or tumor.

paraphrasing: A basic attending skill, or clarifying technique, in which counselors restate in their own words what was just said by the client.

rapport: A special type of bonding that a counselor seeks with a client. The more rapport there is between client and counselor, the greater the client's sense of trust and security.

reel therapy: The use of movies to aid clients in understanding and resolving their own issues.

reflection: The best way to show emotional empathy for a client; the counselor points out the client's emotions by stating them as either seen or heard.

reframing: A therapeutic restatement of a problem that helps the client see the situation differently, usually in a way that makes it easier to solve.

resources: Sources of help in the community. A crisis worker must be knowledgeable about community resources to be able to connect a client in crisis with the appropriate support group or other service.

schizophrenia: A disorder usually requiring the attention of a psychiatrist and characterized by the following symptoms: hallucinations, delusions, loose associations, blunt affect, and poor appearance.

support statements: Therapeutic statements that make clients feel validated and that the counselor truly understands and empathizes with their situation.

support systems: Networks of helping individuals and agencies. A crisis worker uses the client's natural support systems, such as family and friends, and also helps the client build new support systems.

summarization: A skill useful in tying ideas together, wrapping up a session, or moving from the B phase of the ABC model to the C phase; the skill is also useful when the counselor does not know where to go next. It is a statement that pulls together the various facts and feelings discussed in the session.

To sum up the ABC model, a sample script is presented in Table 4.3. This gives readers an idea of the types of questions to ask and statements to make when using the ABC model. The steps of the model are repeated in the table. In each section, please note the specific words (italicized) that a counselor might say to a client.

TABLE 4.3 ABC Model of Crisis Intervention (Sample Script)

A: BASIC ATTENDING SKILLS

What brings you in today? You seem to be having a little trouble getting started. So your girlfriend told you she wants to break up last week and things haven't been going too well lately. You look like you are very sad.

B: IDENTIFYING THE PROBLEM AND THERAPEUTIC INTERACTION
Identify the Precipitating Event:

What specifically brought you in today? Did something happen recently, something different?
Explore Meanings, Cognitions, and Perceptions:

How do you think about it? What does it mean to you? What thoughts go through your mind when you picture the event? How do you put it together in your head? What is it like for you? What specifically do you mean? What are your perceptions about it (the precipitating event)?

Identify Subjective Distress (Emotional Distress):

How do you feel? What emotions are going on inside you? You seem sad, angry, ambivalent, in pain. How have you been feeling since (the precipitating event)?

Identify Impairments in Functioning in the Following Areas:

1. Behavioral

How have you been doing in your life? How are you sleeping? How is your appetite? Have you been carrying on with your normal activities?

2. Social

How are your relationships with your friends and family? Have you been seeing anyone socially since (the precipitating event)? How do you feel or act around people?

3. Academic

Are you going to school? How are your grades lately? Have you been able to study and concentrate in classes? How are you getting along with classmates?

4. Occupational

How are you doing at work? Has your work performance changed since (the precipitating event)? Have you been able to function adequately at work?

Identify Precrisis Level of Functioning in 1–4 Above:

How has your ability to function socially, at school, and at work changed since (the precipitating event)? What was it like for you before (the precipitating event)? What/how were your relationships before (the precipitating event)?

Identify Any Ethical Concerns:

1. Suicide assessment

Have you been thinking about hurting yourself? Have you attempted to kill yourself? Do you want to commit suicide? Do you have a plan? Do you have the means? What is stopping you from killing yourself?

2. Child abuse, elder abuse, homicide

Are your children in danger? Have you or your husband ever caused physical harm to your children? How hard do you hit your kids? How often do you leave your child alone? Have your kids gone without food for an entire day? Has your elderly parent been hurt by the retirement home? When did you first learn that your sister was stealing from your father? How often do you have thoughts about killing your wife? Have you ever hurt someone in the past? How strong are your feelings of murder?

3. Organic or other medical concerns

Are you able to get up in the morning and feed yourself? How many hours do you sleep? Can you dress yourself every day? Do you ever hear voices? Does it ever feel like the phone wires are talking to you? Do you have special powers? Can people read your mind or put thoughts into your head? Do you think people are out to get you? Do you smell or taste things that are unusual?

4. Identify Substance Abuse Issues:

What kinds of drugs have you used in the past? How much alcohol do you drink per week/month/day? What drugs do you use recreationally?

Use Therapeutic Interactions:

1. **Educational comments**
* *Although you feel as though you are the only woman who stays in a battering relationship, it is estimated that about 30 percent of women in the United States live in ongoing battering relationships. Going through a period of intense anger is quite normal and to be expected after the death of a loved one.*
* *Actually, it is not uncommon to be raped by someone you know. Date rape is extremely common for women ages 15–24.*
* *Studies to date do not show that one can catch HIV by shaking hands.*
* *It is not uncommon for the spouse of an alcoholic to be highly anxious about the spouse's drinking.*

2. **Empowerment statements**
* *It is true that you did not have a choice about being raped, but you do have choices now, including whether to press charges, get a medical exam, or drop the whole matter.*
* *Unfortunately, you cannot control your wife's drug use, but you can control your own behavior with her.*
* *True, you are HIV infected and cannot change that. You can, however, choose how to live the rest of your life.*

3. **Support statements**
* *This is an extremely difficult situation, and I don't take it lightly. I can only imagine the pain you are going through. I am so sorry this happened to you.*
* Please, let me be there for you; I care. It must feel pretty bad if you want to kill yourself. These kinds of traumas often make people feel like giving up.

4. **Reframes**
   I think it takes a lot of strength to cry, and I don't see crying as a sign of weakness. Although you see suicide as a sign of strength, it is actually the easy way out of a life filled with difficulties for us all. Staying with a batterer for the sake of your children is evidence of your strength, not a sign of weakness. (Please see each chapter for more examples of reframing.)

C: COPING

IDENTIFY CLIENT'S CURRENT COPING WISHES AND ATTEMPTS:
What would you like to do now to try to cope with your situation? What have you done to try to feel better? What else have you done? Anything else?
Encourage Client to Think of Other Coping Strategies:
What else can you think of to try to get through this? What have you done in the past to get through difficult times? What would you tell a friend to do in this case?

Present Alternative Coping Ideas:

1. **Refer to support groups, twelve-step groups**
   You said you feel better when you talk to friends; how would you feel about attending a support group with other people in your situation? I know of a very special group where people going through what you are going through meet to learn ways to deal with it. Will you give it a try? You can go for as long as you need to, and it is free.

2. **Refer to long-term therapy, family therapy**

   I believe you could benefit most by going to a family therapist/marital thera-pist. Would you consider this? It appears that your problems are longstand-ing. I think longer-term therapy would be really good for you. I know several great counselors. I'll give you a list.

3. **Refer to medical doctor or psychiatrist**

   I would feel most comfortable if you would see a physician. Your symptoms seem serious, and you may need medication or a physical. Do you know of a doctor, or shall I refer you to one that I really respect and work with on other cases?

4. **Legal referral**

   I think you should get legal advice from an attorney. These matters are be-yond my scope of expertise. Please go to the public defender today or to-morrow. Are you aware of restraining orders? You can find out about them at the district attorney's office.

5. **Refer to shelter, other agency**

   How would you feel about going to a battered woman's/homeless shelter? You will be safe there.

6. **Recommend reading books and keeping a journal**

   Do you like to read? I know of some really good books that help explain more about what you are going through. Here is a list of books I recommend for you to read. You said you like to write and have kept a diary before. Many clients feel more under control if they keep a journal while going through difficult times.

Obtain Commitment; Do Follow-up:

When can you make another appointment with me? Call me when you set up your ap-pointment with Dr. Jones. I am going to call you tomorrow. Will you promise not to hurt yourself until you at least speak to me first?

Chapter 6

Cultural Sensitivity in Crisis Intervention

_____ 1. Latino and Hispanic are often used synonymously.

_____ 2. Ataque de Nervios is an example of a culture-bound syndrome.

_____ 3. Etic issues refer to behaviors particular to a cultural group.

_____ 4. Emic issues refer to universal issues.

_____ 5. Asians often deal with issues related to shame and obligation.

_____ 6. African Americans have suffered from racism due to salient differences from mainstream physical appearances.

_____ 7. People within the LGBT subculture are usually seriously mentally ill.

_____ 8. Learning to be culturally sensitive comes naturally to most counselors.

_____ 9. Enmeshed family structures are normal in most Latino families.

_____ 10. Coming out is often a crisis point for a gay individual.

Interest in the sensitivity of counselors and therapists to culturally diverse clients has been growing in the past few decades. It began in the 1960s when the civil rights and affirmative action movements emerged, and became a part of formal education in the late 1980s and 1990s. Arredondo and colleagues (1996, p. 43) describe specific behaviors and attitudes of culturally aware counselors: "Multicultural counseling refers to preparation and practices that integrate multicultural and culture-specific awareness, knowledge, and skills into counseling interactions." They suggest that multicultural refers to five major cultural groups in the United States: African Americans, Asian Americans, Caucasians, Latinos, and Native Americans. The reader is encouraged to obtain a copy of their article and keep it for reference. Although these groups have been the main focus of multicultural studies, other subgroups such as people with disabilities; gays, lesbians, bisexuals, and transgenders; and certain religious groups also have special needs.

The intent of this chapter is to teach readers how to look at certain groups so they can form a working model that will help them understand the norms and family structures of the groups, crises that often arise, and interventions that will alleviate them. Cultural sensitivity is an ethical mandate, and it helps to strengthen clinical practice.

Development of Culturally Sensitive Psychotherapists

As part of a course in a doctoral program at the University of Southern California during the mid 1980s, seven students coauthored an article that describes the **development of cultural sensitivity** in therapists. The students and their professor found similar patterns as all of them struggled with the gender and ethnic issues involved in diagnosing and treating various groups. At that time, very little emphasis had been placed on cultural sensitivity training in graduate programs, so this topic was somewhat novel to most of the students. Based on case vignettes and class discussion, a model of developmental stages was created and is shown in Table 6.1. What was discovered was that learning to be a culturally sensitive counselor is not an easy task. It is normal for counselors to strugggle with developing this type of sensitivity. Counselors do not have to be perfect models of cultural sensitivity, but they are encouraged to be aware of cultural, ethnic, religious, and gender issues that may affect the crisis intervention process.

Knowing about various cultures before meeting with clients can be helpful. It is more important, however, to follow a client's lead in these matters, in order to help the client feel understood and validated. If a counselor fails to respect cultural differences, the crisis intervention may come to an end. In

TABLE 6.1   Proposed Stages and State-Specific Consequences in Therapists'
Development of Cultural Sensitivity

Stage	Description	Consequence
Unawareness of cultural issues	Therapist does not consider a cultural hypothesis in diagnosis.	Therapist does not understand the significance of the clients' cultural background to their functioning.
Heightened awareness of culture	Therapist is aware that cultural factors are important in fully understanding clients.	Therapist feels unprepared to work with culturally different clients; frequently applies own perception of clients' cultural background and therefore fails to understand the cultural significance for a specific client; can at times accurately recognize the influence of clients' cultural background on their functioning.
Burden of considering culture	Therapist is hypervigilant in identifying cultural factors and is, at times, confused in determining the cultural significance of clients' actions.	Therapist believes that consideration of culture is perceived as detracting from his or her clinical effectiveness.
Movement toward cultural sensitivity	Therapist entertains cultural hypotheses and carefully tests these hypotheses from multiple sources before accepting cultural explanations.	Therapist has increased likelihood of accurately understanding the role of culture on clients' functioning.

Source: Lopez et al. (1989). ©1989 by the American Psychological Association. Adapted with permission.

the following case example, the therapist did not show cultural sensitivity, with the consequence that the client dropped out of therapy prematurely.

Unfortunately, counselors are not always culturally sensitive and it this can have deleterious effects on the therapeutic relationship. Box 6.1 presents a case in which the counselor did not use cultural sensitivity.

Etic vs. Emic Issues

In order to help reduce this struggle, various theories regarding how to conceptualize the needs of various cultural groups have been discussed. One way in which to conceptualize how to become culturally sensitive is to understand the difference between etic and emic issues for various cultural groups. **Etic** refers to behaviors and traditions of all or most humans regardless of race, ethnicity, or culture. **Emic** refers to behaviors and traditions particular to a

---

Box 6.1   Example of Lack of Cultural Sensitivity

Example: "A 41-year-old man requested an emergency session regarding his marriage. At his request, I saw him Saturday morning. The man spoke with an Asian accent and said that he was half-Chinese and half-Spanish and had been born in China. As we discussed his presenting problem, the client resisted any of my suggestions that part of his problem might be that his wife was Caucasian, and her parents and siblings disapproved of him. He had come to my office to appease his wife, who said she would leave him unless he sought counseling. The couple had a poor sex life, but he resisted discussing this openly. He kept insisting that the problem was him, and he described himself as a cold person who did not like to be around people.

I noticed myself becoming very frustrated. The client refused to accept the idea that he and his wife had a relationship problem. I guess the client sensed my frustration because he asked if I could refer him to another therapist. He had many demands regarding the times he was available for appointments. He refused marital therapy, which I recommended. I guessed that some of his issues were cultural in nature, but, unfortunately, I will not have the opportunity to explore these issues with him". (Lopez et al., 1989, p. 370)

This vignette indicated that the therapist did not consider cultural factors in her work with this ethnic minority client. She appears to be defining the problem for the client without considering the client's definition of the problem and working from there. This is not to say that the therapist is wrong in her assessment; the client is likely having marital problems. However, her failure to validate his explanatory model or interpretation of the problem may have led to his request for another therapist. (Lopez et al., 1989, p. 371)

---

certain cultural group. The goal is not to use cultural norms to justify behaviors, especially if they are abusive, but to understand and find effective interventions that won't be resisted by the clients. Lastly, it is important to keep in mind that just because certain behaviors and traditions are culturally normal and accepted, it doesn't mean that people in that culture approve of them. In fact, these traditions may be the source of a crisis. This becomes particularly evident when individuals in a family are at different levels of acculturation to mainstream culture.

After a presentation of three ethnic cultural groups, there will be an example of how to look at domestic violence from both an etic and emic perspective, keeping in mind the particular traditions and values of these three groups. Some of the most salient emic traditions and values of Latinos, African-Americans, and Asian Americans will be described in the following section. Following the etic/emic example related to these ethnic groups, the remainder of the chapter focuses on the issues and crises facing individuals who identify with the subgroup of lesbians, gays, bisexuals, and transgenders.

Latinos

The terms *Hispanic, Latino,* and *of Spanish descent* all refer to people whose culture was influenced by the Spanish conquerors of the 15th and 16th centuries. **Hispanic** is an umbrella term for descendants of the colonized natives, Hispanos, and descendants of foreigners and political and economic refugees. **Latino** refers to people from Latin America, which is actually Central and South America. Although there are differences between the various Latino groups, certain similarities exist as well. The most notable commonality is the Spanish language. Language influences thoughts and behaviors, and, therefore, many Latino groups have similar customs. The Spanish influence is also evident in many of their cultural patterns.

About 35.3 million Latinos reside in the United States. They are by far the largest minority group (U.S. Bureau of the Census, 2001). They range from Mexican Americans, to Puerto Rican Americans, to Cuban Americans, to Central and South Americans. Over 10 million live in California, a state that borders Mexico, and was at one time a territory of Mexico. Many Mexican traditions are alive and well in the coastal state. About 6.6 million Latinos live in Texas, and about 2.8 million in New York. Florida has 2.6 million, Illinois 1.5 million, and Arizona 1.2 million. New Mexico is home to 765,386, which is 42 percent of the total population of the state. Because Mexican Americans are the largest group of Latinos in the United States (about 58.5 percent of all Latinos), many counselors find it helpful to understand a little about Mexican American culture.

Mexican American Cultural Patterns

One Mexican cultural behavior that may differ from Anglo-American norms can be observed in child-rearing practices. In Anglo-American culture, autonomy is stressed; in Mexican culture, however, nurturance and obedience to authority are stressed. Mexican American children may sometimesappear to be delayed developmentally. For example, a five-year-old may sit on his mother's lap; a three-year-old may drink out of a bottle; and a 14-year-old may spend all her time with her mother. However, these behaviors are all considered normal in Mexican American culture.

Physical distance between people is another difference. By mainstream American standards, **Mexican Americans** might seem overinvolved with, **enmeshed** with, or overprotective of one another. It is normal, however, for family members to sit close together or to assume that they are to be included in any individual family member's crisis (McGoldrick, Pearce, & Giordana, 2005). Because family closeness is such an important part of Latino culture, crisis workers should keep the **role of systems theory** in mind when working with Mexican American families.

An example of this Latino cultural norm in contrast with mainstream norms might be seen in the case of a Latino daughter who is raped or battered. In such a case, it is likely that each young woman's family will become involved in helping her through the crisis, after she has openly shared her distress with them . This is not to say they will tell her to leave her husband or go to trial for the rape. In contrast, many victims in mainstream American culture deal with these crises with the help of professionals and community support groups without telling their families about their problems.

Mexican American families sometimes do not seek help because they do not know about community resources (McGoldrick, Pearce, & Giordana, 2005). Language barriers, racism, or lack of knowledge may keep them from using even the most basic services available. Workers should not try to conduct long-term introspective, psychodynamic psychotherapy (which, by the way, is counter to most Mexican American norms). Instead, workers should serve as "brokers" for services. This is often an extremely helpful role for a counselor who is working with a Mexican American family in crisis.

In some families, the children are bilingual, but a parent speaks only Spanish. Children may not get the services they need because the parents feel embarrassed or frustrated when they try to explain their needs to professionals and agencies. Often, the job of a crisis worker is to make contact with a school official or a legal advocacy program and connect a family with these services.

Other Cultural Patterns Typical of Latinos   Personalismo is a cultural pattern of relating to others in a manner that may include exaggerated warmth and emotions and a strong need for rapport in order to feel safe or trust others. It is particularly important for crisis workers to grasp this concept when working with Latinos because developing trust is a hallmark process in the helping relationship. Workers may have to spend time in seemingly idle chit-chat. The Latino culture is much more relationship-oriented than task-oriented, unlike mainstream American culture.

Marianisma is a tradition in which the Latina female is expected to be pure and self-sacrificing, focusing more on her children and spouse than her own needs. This contradicts mainstream culture in which women are encouraged to be equal to men and to embrace their own womanhood and personal identity. Sometimes Latina girls raised in the United States reject this quality, creating conflict with their mothers who strongly teach these daughters to be more traditional mothers, wives, and housekeepers. When the daughters do not speak up to their mothers about how this makes them feel depressed, they may be prone to suicide. According to a 2007 Centers for Disease Control and Prevention survey (Yager, 2009), one out of every seven Latina teens, attempts suicide. This is higher than Caucasians (7 percent) and blacks (9 percent).

Machismo is the tradition of the male Latino taking pride in being virile and protective of his family. Many misdefine this quality and think of it as the right for Latino males to be abusive to their wives. True, there may be a strong sense of male privilege in this cutlure, but true machismo means that the man takes care of his wife, not abuses her. This is an effective reframe when a Latino male attempts to justify spousal abuse. It might also be the reason for high rates of drinking, domestic violence, teen pregnancy, and sexual abuse of daughters found in this culture.

Catholicism is still the religion of choice for most Latinos, though many are choosing more fundamental Christian religions than in the past. This

Catholic tradition has in part been a contributing factor to the high rates of teen pregnancy, large families, and very few divorces found in this cultural group. Crisis workers might not assume every Latino is Catholic. It's always a good idea to find out from clients what aspects of their culture are affecting their crisis. In fact, this principle should guide all counseling.

Familismo refers to the value of family above all. This may cause resistance in some Latinos to talk negatively about their family. Also, they may not have many outside support people, and may feel awkward in support groups. Family counseling is an effective style for Latinso when family issues cause the crisis.

Enmeshed family structure is more notable in Latino homes than in mainstream homes. This style of relating gives very little independence to children. Although much emotional support might be present, teens may rebel against this lack of privacy and act out through joing gangs, engaging in sexual acitvities, or attempting suicide.

One last characteristic of Latinos is their tendency toward **emotionalism**, even exaggerated expression that borders on the dramatic. If given the chance, and if they feel safe, they often express their feelings openly in counseling. This expression of affect(emotion)may allow them to master their feelings. Caplan discussed this process when he proposed seven characteristics of people coping effectively. At times, crisis workers may just want to allow clients to express their feelings and not pressure them to solve a problem.

Issues Related to Different Rates of Acculturation

Other crises that may emerge in Mexican American families may reflect patterns that developed and were functional when the family first immigrated to the United States, but have since become restrictive for certain family members. For example, many parents depend on their children to be their intermediaries with the larger culture. When the children grow up and want to separate from their parents, the parents may find it difficult to let them go (McGoldrick, Pearce, & Giordana, 2005).

Adolescents may adopt Anglo values that are contrary to traditional Mexican values. Rejection of parents' cultural values may precipitate a crisis between an adolescent and a Mexican American mother or father. Box 6.2 provides an example of a case in which different rates of acculturation might create problems in a Latino family.

A teenager who joins a gang is acting in a way that is related to different rates of acculturation. Adolescents in general are seeking an identity. Latino teens often feel confused as to whether they should adopt a traditional Latino identiy which sometimes manifests in an "oppressed servant mentality" which might be rejected by a more acculturated teen. Unfortunately, many Hispanic youth choose to adopt a gang mentality/identity in order to feel like they beglong to some type of Latino group in which they can feel respected. Too often these gangs engage in illegal behaviors and encourage the youth to reject their families and schools leading to various crises in the family and within the teen.

Box 6.2   Example of an Adolescent Rejecting Latino Culture

Example: A 15-year-old girl may act out rebelliously by dating boys, staying out late, or dressing less than modestly. A crisis interventionist may suggest that the parents take a more active role in their daughter's maturing by structuring traditional activities for her, such as a *quincinera* (a party to announce entrance to womanhood). The girl's acting-out behavior can then be reframed as confusion about whether she is growing up. A structured ritual will help everyone to more easily accept role changes and should help reduce the family's distress. (McGoldrick, Pearce, & Giordana, 2005)

Using negotiation skills and finding compromises is essential for the interventionist working with dual-culture families. Remember that the parents have chosen to live in the United States; this decision says something about their desire to be connected with some parts of American culture. A counselor can weave this idea into positive reframing, pointing out the opportunity afforded the family that adopts certain Anglo behavioral norms. Studies have shown that emotional distress is higher in Latinos who have either adopted American cultural norms altogether or have totally held onto traditional Mexican cultural norms (Hovey, 2000; McQueen, Getz, & Bray, 2003). Maintaining a bicultural identity seems to be the healthiest mental position for Latinos, and it should be encouraged by mental health clinicians.

Comparison of Mainstream Cultural Values and Latino Resistance in the Mental Health Field

Most theories and techniques in the counseling profession developed within an Anglo-Saxon value system. The three major camps that have traditionally defined mental health and emotional dysfunction are the behavioral, psychoanalytic, and humanistic systems. If crisis workers depend on these traditional theories when working with Latinos, they may encounter much resistance. Table 6.2 presents traditional mainstream values as related to these traditional models and possible Latino resistance to them.

Although these traditional approaches do not appear to be applicable to the Latino population, approaches do exist that are more amenable to their needs. In a 2001 research study (Kanel), 268 Latinos were asked what type of mental health services they would prefer. Of the individuals surveyed, 163 were low-skilled factory workers, most of whom spoke little English. The other 105 individuals were students at a local community college who were learning English or fulfilling general education requirements. The vast majority said they would seek out a counselor if they had family problems (67.2 percent) or if they had their own emotional problems (63.1 percent). Depression and nervousness were the problems for which they would be most likely to seek help (26.9 percent and 24.3 percent, respectively). Other problems that would precipitate a visit to a counselor included "out-of-control anger" (17.2 percent); marriage problems (18.7 percent); disobedient children (16 percent); anxiety (15.3 percent); children's school issues (15.3 percent); and drug problems (15.4 percent).

TABLE 6.2 Comparison of Mainstream and Latino Values in the Mental Health Field

Mainstream Theoretical Model	Latino Resistance
Behavioral Approaches to Parenting	
Behavior modification:	
a. Positive reinforcement or rewards	*Respeto:* Children should do what parents tell them to just because they are children.
b. Response cost	Punishment is considered a form of love and a way to avoid spoiling children.
c. Active parenting approach	Indirect, guilt-inducing methods are commonly used with teens; parenting is not active but assumed.
d. Plan for future parenting	Deal with parenting when it comes; present orientation.
Psychoanalytic Approaches to Parenting	
Stages of development move from complete dependence to complete independence:	
a. Complete dependence	Complete dependence lasts as long as possible.
b. First independence, mobility, self-feeding, bowel control	Physically: Some children are bottle-fed or nursed until they are 5 years old; even preschoolers may be hand-fed.
c. Social independence	Socially: Children have few friends outside the home; they play with siblings and cousins. Children do not have sleepovers. Intrafamilial dependence is normal.
d. Moral independence	Morally: Law and order are valued; children should do what authority says; they are not encouraged to make decisions on their own.
e. Emotional independence	Emotionally: Interdependence with parents and enmeshed boundaries are normal; children are expected to meet their parents' needs.
Humanistic and Existential Approaches to Parenting	
a. Self-awareness	Denial of relational conflicts; anxiety with self-awareness
b. Confrontation in relational conflicts	Avoidance of confrontation
c. Genuine encounters and intimacy	Lack of intimacy and authentic relating; interactions are prescribed and based on hierarchy and gender roles.

Source: This table is the original work of Kanel, 2003.

When asked about the way they would want the counselor to relate to them, 35.8 percent said they would prefer to have the counselor give a lot of advice, 26.5 percent stated they wanted the counselor to ask a lot of questions; 21.6 percent preferred the counselor to be personal; and 50.4 percent wanted the counselor to be very professional. Interestingly, although 63.8 percent believed that talking about their childhood would help resolve current problems, only 18.3 percent stated they would want to talk about their childhood; 66.4 percent preferred to talk about current problems. As for the use of medication, 59% did not believe it could help them with their problems, and only 7.8 percent preferred to take medication to resolve emotional problems.

The author simultaneously surveyed 43 Spanish-speaking therapists in southern California on their treatment of this population. When asked about the type of intervention they use with Spanish-speaking clients, 28 percent said cognitive-behavioral therapy, 26 percent said family counseling, 23 percent said psychoeducational therapy, and 23 percent said referrals to other agencies. These approaches in combination are the same as the crisis intervention model presented in this book.

Based on these results and Latino cultural norms, it appears that two approaches would be most effective: the family system model and the crisis intervention model (which is heavily influenced by cognitive, behavioral, and psychoeducational models).

Ataque de Nervios

One Latino phenomenon that may come to the crisis worker's attention is **ataque de nervios (los nervios)**, which literally means "attack of nerves." This is a culture-bound, self-labeled syndrome found only in Latinos. It is often a reaction to trauma, death, marital infidelity, or family conflict. A person suffering from this may seek help from a physician, counselor, or curandero (folk healer). Symptoms include panic attacks, fits of violent agitation with self-mutilation and suicidal behavior (Schechter et al., 2000, p. 530), shaking, heart palpitations, numbness, shouting, swearing, striking others, falling, convulsions (Liebowitz et al., 1994, p. 871), and signs of dissociation (Oquendo, 1995).

In 2004, the author conducted a study of 198 Latinos whose dominant language was Spanish, and 37 mental health clinicians who treat Spanish-speaking clients to better understand ataque de nervios and treat it. Mental health counselors have been confused about how best to diagnose this disorder and how to intervene when it occurs. The two main symptoms reported by participants were screaming and despair. Being out of control, crying, and feeling irritable and anxious were mentioned frequently as well. Crisis workers may attribute these symptoms to panic disorder, generalized anxiety disorder, or depression. Of the Latinos surveyed, 76 percent reported symptoms of ataque de nervios that could fit more than two diagnoses or would not fit any diagnosis. Others have reported confusion in diagnosing ataque de nervios when using the universally accepted nomenclature of the DSM-IV, developed by the American Psychiatric Association in 1994. None of those studies resulted in an exact fit with traditional diagnoses, either, and most recommended further study to better understand the relationships between ataque de nervios and other disorders (Koss-Chioino, 1999; Liebowitz et al., 1994; Oquendo, 1995; Schechter et al., 2000).

What then are the implications for the crisis worker when a client presents with ataque de nervios? Both groups in the author's 2004 study overwhelmingly selected family conflicts (76 percent of Latinos and 82 percent of clinicians) as the number one cause. Emotional problems and work conflicts were mentioned as the next two causes by the Latino group. Clinicians reported that drug and alcohol abuse, childhood abuse, and intrapsychic conflict were also important causes. Only 26 percent of clinicians stated that the cause was a biochemical imbalance. This is important information because people suffering from ataque de nervios are usually diagnosed as having biochemical imbalances and given medication as the treatment of choice. According to the study, however, the causes are interpersonal and psychological and, therefore, need psychological treatment and family therapy. Although medication may help, it is not sufficient. In fact, curanderos may help clients more than therapists if clients believe in the power of herbal cleansing or faith healing.

When Latinos present with ataque de nervios, crisis workers would be wise to use the ABC model, giving the client plenty of time to express feelings. Helping the client feel understood is vital for him or her to overcome the sense of being out of control. Family sessions are helpful. The focus should be on developing new ways to cope with stress in relation to family members and co-workers. If the symptoms are extremely debilitating, referral to a physician may be warranted. In the study, 31 percent of Latinos stated that they talked to family and friends to overcome ataque de nervios, 21 percent saw a therapist, 21 percent received medication from a physician, 17 percent said the condition went away by itself, 12 percent received medication from a psychiatrist, 10 percent saw a curandero, and 14 percent used folk remedies such as smelling onions, prayer, and hands-on healing. Of the clinicians surveyed, 60 percent used cognitive therapy, 56 percent supportive therapy, and 48 percent family therapy; 43 percent recommended using medication; and only 0.08 percent used expressive or psychoanalytic therapy.

African American Families

In an ideal world, people would pay no attention to skin color. However, if mental health providers do not realize that **African American** culture differs in various ways from mainstream American culture, they may do a disservice to this group.

When one considers the history of African Americans, one can understand their family structure and value systems. African Americans who were raised in slavery learned to exist in settings where roles were flexible and families usually extended to several generations. These aspects can be readily seen in modern-day African American families. Elderly people as well as young adults "tend

---

Box 6.3   Example of Emic Needs in an African American Household

Example: A child may be brought in by his parents for misbehaving in school. You may discover that the parents do not understand his behavior and seem to be ineffective in eliminating it. Perhaps the child's grandmother is perceived by all to be the primary disciplinarian and nurturer. Instead of taking those responsibilities away from the grandmother and giving them to the parents (which would disengage the grandmother from the problem), you may want to bring the grandmother into the sessions and work with her alongside the parents. You would be culturally biased if you insisted that only the parents be involved in the child's therapy.

---

to be supported by the collective efforts of family members both within and outside the nuclear family" (McGoldrick, Pearce, & Giordana, 2005). This history certainly has implications for the crisis interventionist. The worker can use naturally existing support systems for each individual. The worker will also explore the role norms of the person's family system so he or she does not see a problem when none exists, which is true of all cultural groups. Box 6.3 above provides an example of the extended family support system in the African American culture and how a crisis worker might utilize this cultural tradition.

Role of Religion in African American Life

Slaves found solace in the view that God would provide a better world for them after they had left this world of suffering. This tradition of strong religious beliefs and practices has been passed down through the generations and must be kept in mind by the crisis worker.

The church has been a forum in which many African American women and men have expressed their talents and leadership skills (McGoldrick, Pearce, & Giordana, 2005) and have found a kind of haven from a racist society. For the crisis interventionist, incorporating the church into therapy, either by seeking support from a minister or by encouraging the client to become involved in church activities, is valuable. Many African Americans do not place much trust in mainstream, middle-class mental health counselors. African American ministers, however, often do trust counselors and may be able to allay the fears of parishioners who would benefit from counseling.

Sometimes, appeals for help from the church are not productive. If clients are extremely mistrustful of counselors, one can empathize with the distrust and help clients engage with traditional cultural support systems that they do trust, such as family and friends. Unfair treatment of African Americans by the legal system is well documented; a disturbing encounter with the system is one event that may lead to a family crisis.

Problem-Solving Model for African Americans

Not all African American families in crisis need to be referred to traditional support systems. A growing number have adopted mainstream, middle-class values and will respond to crisis intervention. Focusing on the presenting problems and setting up goal-specific plans often work well. Some African Americans will seek out and accept insight-oriented therapy. The most important goal is to determine the needs of a particular client or family and meet these needs with cultural sensitivity. The worker must always acknowledge that racism is present in our society and must try to understand the world of a client who deals with racism every day. Because most African Americans speak English, the differences in any cultural traditions aren't related to language. In fact, African Americans have lived in the United States longer than many other ethnic groups who immigrated during the late 1800s, so they are usually acculturated to mainstream values such as independence, self-reliance, rights, and equality as much as most Caucasians.

Wright (1993) emphasizes the importance of cultural sensitivity when a worker has an African American male client who is dealing with issues of sexual behavior and the risk of HIV infection or AIDS. His research shows that African American men may have different views about sexual categories and behavior than Caucasian men. AIDS is widespread among African Americans and is primarily spread by men. Therefore, intervention strategies must be sensitive to the values and behaviors of African American men.

Wright suggests that current educational materials, health facilities, and community-based AIDS education and prevention programs are inadequate in their cultural and racial sensitivity. He states that "the AIDS epidemic is not merely a medical dilemma but is a socio-cultural medical dilemma. For African American men, AIDS has become an overwhelming and devastating blow that has torn away at their already threatened health and social status" (Wright, 1993, p. 430). Wright recommends that future policies should address cultural issues when programs are created to help prevent and reduce the risk of AIDS transmission among African Americans.

Although this research focuses on social policy, individual crisis workers can also benefit from these studies of the sexual behavior of African American men. Crisis workers can realize that for this group, a person's sexual behavior does not necessarily cause the person to be labeled a homosexual, heterosexual, or bisexual. Asking questions such as "Are you gay?" to see if a person is at risk for AIDS would be inappropriate, because even though a man may be engaging in homosexual behavior, he may not regard himself as a homosexual. (This is true for any client, not just African American clients.) It would be more suitable to identify specific behaviors that are associated with a high risk of AIDS and to provide information about such behaviors and about ways to prevent transmission of HIV. (See Chapter 12 for more details.) Once a worker understands the client's perspective, the worker has accomplished the most important part of his or her task. Using this knowledge to help the person cope is the next challenge.

Asian American Families

Asian American families have their roots in East Asia—China, Japan, and Korea—which is an area distinguished by having the oldest continually recorded civilization in the world. Its history gives it a background very different from that of the West in a variety of ways. For example, there are differences in philosophical approaches to life that are dictated in the East by Confucianism and Buddhism rather than Judeo-Christianity. Eastern systems do not stress independence and autonomy but rather emphasize the importance of the family and the specific hierarchical roles established for all members. Rules for behavior are extremely strong and more formalized than in other cultures. Because these people lived for years under oppressive dynastic rule and needed to maintain a large labor force capable of heavy manual and agricultural labor, male offspring became more valued than female offspring (McGoldrick, Pearce, & Giordana,2005).

There are historical differences between the various Asian cultures. Language is one difference; another is the specific immigration problems and circumstances that each group experienced. Many Vietnamese people fled in boats to escape Communist rule. Many Japanese people came to America to take advantage of financial investments and employment opportunities.

Crisis Intervention Issues for Asian Americans

Although not all persons of Asian descent react the same, certain characteristics are commonly seen in people in crisis states and those using coping skills. The typical middle-class, Judeo-Christian attitude of many mainstream training programs and work settings in the mental health field often does not address the special needs of Asian Americans.

The idea that the family should be placed ahead of individuals is one cultural difference that can definitely affect the counselor's work. Asian Americans are traditionally taught to respect family needs more than personal needs. Kashiwagi (1993, p. 46) states that "back in the old country the people had to band together, work together cooperatively, just to survive. I think because this value system worked then it was handed down." He further proposes that Asians who came to America felt the need to prove themselves, and this set up the "model minority" stereotype. This tradition of being overachieving, hardworking, and industrious may lead to stress and pressure to maintain the status quo inside and outside the Asian American community. The crisis worker might keep these characteristics in mind when working with this population.

Southeast Asians and Posttraumatic Stress Disorder

Kinzie and his colleagues (1984) have noted certain values held by Southeast Asian clients that affect the course of psychotherapy when they are treated for posttraumatic stress disorder (PTSD):

1. An orientation to the past, including great respect for ancestors
2. A primary reliance on the family as the basis of personal identity and self-esteem
3. The tolerance of multiple belief systems in regard to religion and cosmology and acceptance of life as it is rather than what it could be (pp. 645–646)

The mainstream-oriented crisis worker can consider these values when dealing with this Asian population so as not to force values on them that do not fit with their cultural norms. However, Boehnlein (1987, p. 525) believes that the mainstream cognitive psychotherapeutic approach does have relevance for Cambodian patients with PTSD:

This approach facilitates an ongoing dialogue allowing the therapist to directly address issues in treatment that may relate to conflicting beliefs and values, along with doubts about one's personal and social identities that may affect interpersonal functioning. This is especially helpful in PTSD patients who have such profound doubts about their self-worth and their abilities to make effective changes in their lives based on personal traumatic histories and religious belief systems which often lead to a pessimistic view of fate.

Boehnlein (1987, p. 526) offers some specific questions a crisis worker might ask a Southeast Asian client with PTSD:

"Do you have to attain perfection in order to not consider yourself a failure?" "Given the progress you have steadily been making, is your life still fated to be continuously and forever difficult?"

"You have been viewing yourself as a weak and ineffective person, yet you had the strength as an adolescent to survive years of starvation and brutality. There must be strengths that you and your family possess that you have not been aware of in recent years." [Note that these statements are examples of reframing.]

Boehnlein further notes that these patients tend to minimize outward emotional expression. Persons with PTSD who feel they must not display emotions can use up a lot of psychic energy. Therefore, when working with Asian patients who have PTSD, crisis workers need to be aware of their own affective responses and the subtle cues of internal distress communicated by patients. These cues may be communicated through reports of dreams or perhaps behavioral signs of depression, such as somatic distress or sleep disturbance.

Finally, Boehnlein (p. 527) suggests that the therapist can communicate a sense of warmth, genuineness, and competence by being direct, yet compassionate; by being assertive in the recommendation of treatment approaches, yet responsive to possibly conflicting cultural concepts of illness and healing; and by allowing the patient to report difficult historical information or express intense emotion without a sense of shame. Explaining to patients in a matter-of-fact way that a number of their experiences and feelings are shared by many other Cambodians does not trivialize their personal situation but instead serves to minimize their fear of going crazy. This is a good example of how educational comments and reframing can be used.

In his work with Asian Americans, Hong (1988) has found that mental health workers would do well to adopt a general family practice model whereby they maintain an ongoing interaction with the family and serve as a resource that the family can consult when they are in difficulty. A counselor should use knowledge of the client as well as knowledge of the client's family, community, and social environment. This approach seems particularly suitable for Asian Americans whose culture emphasizes the role of the family.

Box 6.4   Example of Cultural Needs and a Culturally Sensitive Intervention with an Asian Client

Example: A 26-year-old Vietnamese female came for crisis intervention because of her depression and the increasing tension in her house. She was a medical student and working full-time. Her father expected her to serve him, support the family financially, and stay at home when she was not at school or work. Her older brother was permitted to lie around the house, contributing nothing; the client was very angered by this inequality. She realized that she had become quite Anglicized in her value system and felt taken advantage of by her family. She was miserable and pondered suicide.

In analyzing this case, the counselor realized that cultural sensitivity was vital. If the counselor thought only in terms of middle-class, Caucasian values, he would support the separation/individuation process and encourage the client to assert her own needs and rights. However, if this client were to go against the wishes of her father, she would be ostracized from her family. A few concepts can help explain this dilemma.

It helps to minimize the client's inhibition against seeking mental health services, gives the client the advantage of having family support, and helps the client in therapy because there is less resistance from the family system.

Whenever possible, the crisis worker will take into consideration the effect any intervention will have on the client's family. The worker might consider bringing in the family whenever possible. To suggest that a client focus exclusively on her or his own problems will undoubtedly wreak havoc on the family system. A difficult case in which a highly acculturated Asian woman sought crisis intervention is presented in Box 6.4.

Asian American Family Structure

In most traditional Asian families, males are respected more than females. The oldest son has more privileges than his own mother, though he must respect her at certain levels. The mother plays the stereotypical role of nurturer, providing domestic structure, whereas the father dictates all family decisions. The daughter contributes to the household until she marries; then she belongs to her husband's household and family. The concept of individualism is not part of this culture.

Shame and Obligation in Asian American Culture

If the norms are not followed, an individual and the family will experience a sense of shame, not only for their own actions but for the entire family line. This factor makes it necessary at times to reject a family member completely so as not to bring shame on the family. Differentiation between the family as a whole and its members often does not exist as it does in European cultures. Obligation arises in any situation in which the rules of family structure come into play. The child is obligated to respect the structure. If the child does not, he or she will bring shame on the family. Having to choose between obligation and individual freedom often brings on feelings of depression and anxiety. The crisis worker needs to be sensitive to these struggles and search for ways to negotiate compromises when possible.

In the case of the young medical student, the counselor did not suggest that she move out and tell her father that she is an adult and does not have to support him. Instead, the counselor encouraged her to use the counseling sessions as times to vent her frustrations. The crisis worker let the young woman know that she understood her dilemma and that by choosing to maintain the status quo, the woman could continue to be a part of her family. The consequences for violating the system would be complete alienation from her mother and sisters as well as the men in her family. If she could learn to keep her focus on the value of family, perhaps she could learn to let go of her feelings of unfairness. In reframing the situation, the worker pointed out that although the client felt a lot of pressure to keep the family from being shamed, her father felt this obligation even more. In actuality, the father carried the burden of keeping his family in line. He would experience incredible shame if his daughter were to move out while she was unmarried and refuse to support his family financially.

Kashiwagi (1993, p. 46) provides another example of how "certain traditional Asian cultural influences, such as bringing shame to the family and losing face in the community," have an effect on mental health problems and intervention. He asserts that when an Asian American teenager has a drug or alcohol addiction, the family often denies the condition and perpetuates the problem. This denial results in large part from the lack of connection, communication, and understanding in the parent-child relationship. If the counselor recommends a tough love approach—that is, tells the parents to refuse to continue being enablers for the teenager's behavior and set standards that he must meet—the parents probably will not follow through adequately because of the cultural tendency to care for family members at a surface level.

Another example of the importance of avoiding family shame was presented by Carol Cole (1993). In her role as an emergency response worker with a county mental health unit, she received a call from neighbors, who complained of an awful stench coming from a house next door. When she arrived, she found a 40-year-old Asian American woman who was completely psychotic. She was delusional, disheveled, and disoriented, had no food in the house, and showed no signs of reality orientation. Her Asian family had immigrated to the United States five years earlier, and the parents had kept this 40-year-old daughter in the home with no treatment because acknowledging that a child was mentally ill would bring shame on the family. Two weeks earlier, the parents had been in a car wreck, and no one was at home to take care of the daughter. In this case, although the client was hospitalized involuntarily, the action was reframed as an opportunity to help stabilize the daughter and teach the family about available resources—in this case, resources in the Vietnamese community.

Strict approaches that require setting firm limits, such as making a child sleep outside or go to school in dirty clothes, bring shame to the whole family; therefore, parents tend to enable irresponsible behaviors to avoid shame. To confront a child about how her or his behavior makes the family feel would be shameful, so parents' true feelings are often hidden. The child usually knows this, can take advantage of it, and can abuse the parents' acts of kindness. This situation is especially damaging when a child is addicted to drugs. Teenagers know that their parents will bail them out of jail if they are arrested or will always allow them to stay at home. Not to do so would bring shame to the family. Unfortunately, many parents of drug-addicted Asian American teenagers believe they are helping their children by taking care of their basic needs and buying them material things. This, however, reinforces the addicts' behaviors and enables further drug use. The crisis counselor must be sensitive to these cultural norms and slowly encourage open communication between generations rather than force them to take such actions as tough love.

Communication Process in Asian American Culture

Another area in which sensitivity is helpful is communication style. Asian Americans have been conditioned to avoid eye contact and direct confrontations, especially with doctors and authority figures. This trait may create complications during an interview if the counselor is not aware of this cultural style. Whereas mainstream Americans may consider avoiding eye contact to be rude, Asians may feel that looking someone in the eye is rude. Also, Asian clients may feel that they cannot disagree with the counselor because of respect for the authority position. The counselor may have to encourage disagreement and define it as part of the interview process at times.

Also, if a crisis counselor is working with a family, the tendency to ask family members to confront each other directly may be culturally insensitive. They will probably do best with more educational, problem-solving approaches that focus on a presenting problem. Reframing the solution as strengthening the family unit will probably be well received by Asian American clients. The crisis worker might try to be aware of the hierarchy in the family and include the most powerful family members in making decisions. Box 6.5 gives an example of a young man caught in a dilemma due to Asian cultural values.

Box 6.5   Example of Reframing with a Suicidal Asian Man

Example: A 19-year-old Asian American youth was depressed about having received a C in a chemistry course. He felt ashamed and was sure his father would be angry with him for bringing disgrace on the family. He believed that his only solution was to kill himself by jumping off a tall building.

Instead of working only with this client, the counselor would be well advised to bring in the young man's parents. The client can be told that his suicide might bring more shame to the family than getting a C in chemistry. The worker can reframe the problem by pointing out that the lower grade in chemistry could be balanced by a high grade in another class. By asking his parents for their opinions and possible solutions, the client will feel more secure in the fact that he will not bring shame to them. Instead, the family may be brought closer together. The counselor might emphasize to the parents that their son cares so much about the family name that he was willing to sacrifice his own life for the family honor—another reframing of the situation.

TABLE 6.3   Summarization of Special Considerations in Working with Mexican Americans, African Americans, and Asian Americans

Mexican Americans
- Enmeshed family structure
- Language barriers
- Different levels of acculturation
- Strong Catholic religious focus
- Personalismo
- Marianismo
- Machismo
- Familismo

African Americans
- History of racism dating back to era of slavery
- Group with the most salient differences from the mainstream group
- Distrust of mainstream institutions
- Clergy serve as traditional support system when crises arise

Asian Americans
- Shame and obligation
- Rigid family roles and structures
- Counseling should be problem focused and formal

Table 6.3 summarizes salient issues for the crisis worker to remember when working with the three ethnic groups just discussed. The worker is advised to remember, however, that each person is unique and that these issues may not apply to everyone. Most importantly, the worker must remember to understand the crisis experience from the client's point of view.

Example of Etic vs. Emic Issues Relating to Domestic Violence for Three Ethnic Groups

Etic Issues

Men asserting power over women is an historical reality. Since the beginning of human civilization, men have been responsible for the survival of the family unit in large part because of their larger size and superior strength. There may have been a built-in mechanism to ensure aggressivity and survival. It is possible that women learned to be patient and tolerate the man's needs and behaviors in order to ensure she and the children would survive. It was not uncommon for men to raid neighboring tribes and forcibly take women back to live with them with the intent of impregnating them, probably an inherent instinct to propegate the species of Homosapiens. It is likely that a man controlled his mate to ensure she would take care of his children. This history of men asserting dominance over women is probaly a universal reality in most cutlural groups.

While these traditions were universal for many centuries, in today's world, brute strength is not as vital for survival. Men and women are more equal in terms of keeping the family unit alive. It is possible that men haven't caught up to women evolutionarily speaking, hence the high rates of domestic violence throughout all cultures worldwide.

Emic Considerations

Latinos   Isolation may be a particular problem for Latinos who do not speak English and are very unacculturated to mainstream values. These victims of domestic violence often feel disconnected from medical care providers, and recent immigrants may feel threatened to call the police for fear of deportation. These unacculturated Latinas might be unaware of resources available such as shelters and may experience a deeper stigma associated with problems in the family making it difficult to tell others of her abuse. Economic abuse may be a related problem for some unacculturated immigrant Latinas who lack economic self-sufficiency due to poor English, poor employment history, and lack of skills or education. Other issues particular to Latinas may include the Latina tradition of machismo in which males are allowed to assert male privilege over females. Some Latinas might find it hard to discern which behaviors by the man is abuse, and which is normal machismo. Familismo might intensify her desire to maintain the family unity at all costs (Volpp, & Main, 1995; Sorenson, 1996).

African Americans   These abused women might also feel isolated from the outside community due to not wanting to betray her own community and further societal feelings of racism. They may also feel mistrust of the legal system and health care providers due to past experiences of racism. As with many women, African-American women may not have economic self-sufficiency and feel unable to leave a violent situation. Lastly, some African American women who are subject to emotional and physical abuse by a male partner may feel they need to support African American males and not expose him to any more stressors from a racist society (Thompson & Maslow, 2000; White, 1994; Campbell, 1993).

Asian Americans   As with other women, Asian American women often feel isolated from outside communities. Their reluctance to discuss family violence may be due to the fear of bringing shame on their family and ostracism from their own community. They may also have language and other cultural differences, be unaware of basic civil rights afforded them in the United States, and lack resources that are linguistically and culturally appropriate, especially if she is the only surviving refugee of her family. In Asian cultures there also tends to be a norm that encourages gender inequality which is often very visible and pronounced. Men are often seen as superior to make important decisions, and a woman does not usually disagree with her spouse in public (Huisman, 1996; Richie, 1988).

While it seems true that these cultural groups seem to have built-in norms that encourage domestic violence, this does not mean we must support these cultural norms. Counselors can always proceed with the knowledge that domestic violence is a crime and punishable in the United States. The goal is to understand and not judge, and still help both the victims and the perpetrators

---

Box 6.6   Cases to Role Play

Case 1 A Mexican American woman comes to see you because she has been depressed since her last child entered kindergarten. She does not sleep well, is nervous, and fights to get her child to obey her.

What cultural issues are at stake here? How would you proceed?

Hint: Offer psychoeducational information regarding child development.

Hint: Offer supportive statements about letting go of her child.

Hint: Reframe the child's rebelliousness as a sign that the mother has raised a secure child who can function in school.

Hint: Empower the mother by pointing out how her role as a mother has just changed, not been eliminated. She has new tasks to master now, which will be even more challenging than when her child was younger.

Hint: Offer educational information about the possibility of different rates of acculturation as a child enters school.

Case 2 A 19-year-old Vietnamese female college student is distressed because she has fallen in love with an American boy. She wants to spend time with him, but her parents expect her to stay at home when she is not at school. She wants to kill herself because she is so depressed.

How can you help her? What must you keep in mind?

Hint: Offer supportive statements about how difficult it is to respect one's parents and still have one's own life.

Hint: Educate her about the different rates of acculturation of her and her parents.

Hint: Empower her by focusing on what she can do to feel better; talk about ways that she can show respect to her parents and perhaps still see the boy at school.

Hint: Conduct a suicide assessment and discuss the fact that if she killed herself, she would bring more shame on her family than she would by dating a boy.

Hint: Offer to speak with her parents about the situation and let them know how much their daughter respects them—so much that she would rather kill herself than shame them. They would not want her to kill herself over this situation.

Case 3 A 14-year-old African American boy is sent for counseling by his school counselor because he has not been coming to school and is not performing when he is in school. His mother brings him to the appointment. She is in a hurry because she is on her lunch break from her full-time job. His father does not live with them, though he comes around frequently.

Who might be available for support? What biases must you avoid?

Hint: Find out who the teen and his mother live with, and if is there a grandmother available to help out.

Hint: Educate the boy about the need to finish high school and the special importance of this for African Americans, because discrimination is bad enough, even when one has a diploma.

Hint: Encourage the father to be involved in the situation and be a good role model.

Hint: Empathize with the teen about the fact that school is not always easy or fun.

Hint: Assess the teen's level of depression and ask about what has been happening in his life recently.

understand that their lives can be more satisfying without violence. For these ethnic groups, crisis workers can aid both victims and perpetrators in finding ways to fulfill the need for power and control through education, discussion of cutlural norms and why those norms may not be viable within mainstream culture. Helping clients understand the etic and emic of any crisis is often very helpful. This example just focused on domestic violence, but the model may be useful for other struggles they may present.

The Subculture of Gays, Lesbians, Bisexuals, and Transgenders

Terms that are commonly used in discussions of the gay, lesbian, bisexual, and transgender population are listed below. These individuals are sometimes referred to as the g/l/b/t population. The definitions may be helpful to the reader.

bisexual: A person who experiences social and romantic attraction to both genders.

closet gay: A person who is unaware of his or her homosexuality or is unwilling to publicly acknowledge it; such a person may be described as "being in the closet."

coming out: The process of identifying and coming to terms with one's homosexuality. The term is also used to describe a homosexual person who is telling another person that he or she is gay.

gay: A man that is mostly sexually attracted to men.

heterosexism: The attitude of overt or covert bias against homosexuals based on the belief that heterosexuality is superior.

homophobia: Unreasonable fear or hatred of a homosexual.

homosexuality: Sexual desires primarily for a person of the same sex.

lesbian: A woman who feels sexual desire predominantly for other women.

transgender: A person who has experienced himself or herself socially, emotionally, and psychologically as male if the person was born female, or female if the person was born male.

There seems to be a trend among adults toward more acceptance of gays and lesbians in society (Yang, 1999). This is evident in the ratings of television shows that have been nominated for and won Emmy awards, such as *Queer Eye for the Straight Guy* and *Will and Grace*, and in the open disclosure by some celebrities of their homosexual identity. However, many people still have negative feelings toward individuals who live openly gay and lesbian lifestyles. Adults who present themselves to the world as gay make themselves open to criticism and rejection by family, friends, and co-workers. Recent political discussions have highlighted the ongoing debate about whether gays should be allowed to be legally married with the same rights as heterosexual married couples. Proponents of gay marriage believe that not allowing gay marriage is a form of discrimination. This is such an important issue that it has become a platform upon which certain major political parties run.

Keeping one's homosexuality hidden can lead to mental health problems such as anxiety and depression. The closet gay must always worry about keeping his or her true sexual orientation concealed. Often these people must lie to those they care about, and this duplicity leads to negative feelings.

Crisis hot lines and centers have been established to help this population live healthy gay and lesbian lifestyles, disclose their orientation to others, and learn how to handle rejection from society. A counselor is encouraged to be sensitive to the special issues faced by both the closet gay and the openly gay person. It is best to find out how each individual perceives his or her situation and continue with the interview following the ABC model. Knowing about community resources is a big help.

Typical Issues Facing G/L/B/T Persons in Crisis

Unlike other minority groups, when an individual accepts the fact that he or she is gay, lesbian, bisexual, or transgender, he or she usually feels isolated from family and friends. Many times the child grows up in a home where he or she receives messages full of heterosexism (i.e., that the only proper sexual relations are between females and males) and homophobia (i.e., the fear of homosexuality). When individuals begin to recognize themselves as being gay or lesbian, they must also contend with their own homophobia. They often prefer to deny the possibility of being gay or lesbian.

Families of these individuals also experience crises. Parents are not prepared to raise or be involved in the life of a gay child. They often feel like failures and feel guilty about their resentment of their child's sexual orientation. Many parents believe that being gay is an illness and seek treatment for their child's homosexuality, despite the fact that, since 1974, formal psychiatric nomenclature did not include homosexuality as a mental disorder.

Suicide is a big risk for individuals in the beginning stages of discovering their gay sexual orientation as well as for gay persons who experience societal discrimination. The news media often has reports of hate crimes against gays. Gay persons have been socialized in a culture that fears homosexuality on moral grounds. Judeo-Christian culture has emphasized that sodomy is a sin. Therefore, gay individuals often experience self-loathing for a time until they can come to terms with the reality of their sexuality.

Although certain sexual acts, such as sodomy and oral sex, are illegal in some states, being gay is not illegal. In fact, being gay is much more than a sexual act. People who are gay build lives together, build friendship networks, work in many fields, and live productive lives.

Coming Out

Coming out does not happen overnight; it is a process that happens over time. The phrase usually refers to telling someone of one's gay sexual orientation. It is often done in stages rather than as a single event. This process of accepting one's gay sexuality usually begins deep within a person's psyche as he or she experiences feelings, thoughts, and desires related to his or her sexuality. There may be an inner battle as the person fights with cultural homophobic norms. When an individual is socialized to believe that gays are deviants, it is difficult to come to terms with one's own feelings of homosexuality without believing that one is deviant.

The person coming out often contends with shame that he or she imposes on himself or herself or that society imposes on him or her. Fear is a big factor as well. Some of this fear is realistic, as rejection from family and friends is a common consequence of coming out. Each time an individual informs someone that he is gay, he must face the fear of the unknown. Because of societal discrimination, the person may fear losing a job, losing a home (or not being allowed to purchase a home), or losing respect from others. The decision to come out, then, must not be an impulsive act but rather one that is well thought out and strategic. A crisis counselor can assist persons as they move slowly through this process to help reduce negative consequences.

Once there is an internal acceptance of being homosexual, individuals begin the process of reprogramming their ideas about being gay and turn the shame into pride. There may be a phase of experimentation with their new identity when they tell friends and family or connect with the gay community through nightclubs and community centers.

The age of an individual who is coming out makes a difference in the consequences in his or her life. For example, a middle-aged woman who had been married for 15 years and has children will need to think carefully before coming out. It could take several years for her to make the decision to live as a lesbian, even though she clearly experiences her sexuality that way. She must proceed slowly and deal with all the members of her family so as to decrease trauma for everyone. The crisis worker should not encourage people to come out immediately but rather guide clients into their own coming-out process. The counselor may even play devil's advocate and help clients question whether the gay feelings are real. This does not mean that the counselor discourages a person from being gay. It is not a disorder that needs to be fixed but, rather, an identity with social consequences. This fact must be part of crisis intervention.

A 25-year-old woman who lives on her own, has good self-esteem, and can rely on a good support system might have an easier time coming out. However, keep in mind that coming out is probably never easy because of societal taboos, parental reactions, and reactions of friends and co-workers who did not know about the person's gay sexuality. Some people believe that being gay is fine until one of their own loved ones comes out as gay. Family members might go into a state of shock when they find out that a child is gay. In Box 6.7 you will read about a family going through a coming out crisis.

During the coming-out process, there is an increased risk of suicidal thinking and attempts. The individual may feel hopeless about the future; helpless and worthless; and may experience many painful feelings. Add to these

---

Box 6.7   Example of a Coming out Crisis and the Family Reaction

Example: A 17-year-old girl had been struggling with her sexuality for 2 years. She had engaged in moderate lesbian sexual activities with a girl on her basketball team. She kept the truth about this relationship from her parents and said the other girl was just a good friend. The girl finally told her mother that she was bisexual and wanted to date males and females. The mother became hysterical and said that the girl was just confused and would eventually realize she was totally straight. Soon, the girl met another female who was a lesbian. The girl became very involved with her and realized that she was a lesbian herself, not bisexual. She told her mother, who went into shock. All the mother's hopes and dreams about having a big wedding for her daughter and future son-in-law and having grandchildren were lost. The mother could not see that there could still be a future with her daughter. The father disowned the daughter.

---

feelings increased social isolation, and the risk of suicide can be quite high. The crisis worker should evaluate suicide regularly when a client is experiencing this type of crisis, particularly when disclosures are being made and rejection by loved ones is possible.

Remember that there will be consequences when a person comes out. The counselor must not make the decision about when to come out for a client. Instead, the crisis worker should help client make his or her own decision by using empowering and support statements. By discussing the consequences of not coming out, such as emotional repression, unhappiness in relationships, and pervasive guilt and shame, persons considering coming out might be helped to see that the immediate consequences of possible rejection are better than a life of permanent dissatisfaction.

The crisis counselor can say that although friends and family may be rejecting at first, attitudes change over time. Just as clients may not have been able to accept their gay sexuality at first, loved ones may not be accepting, either. Time is an important factor. Support groups are useful. The crisis worker should refer clients to a group in which others can relate to the dilemma firsthand. Being reassured by educational statements that homosexuality is not a disease can often help the client feel better as well. Many communities have gay/lesbian/bisexual/transgender centers that provide services for the many issues facing the gay population. Most colleges have special centers for gay people. Even some high schools have gay and lesbian associations. Crisis workers may also provide family counseling to mediate between children and parents or between spouses. Of course, suicide assessment should be done when clients are depressed.

Transgender people are usually men. They have experienced themselves emotionally, psychologically, and socially as females since childhood, despite having a male body. As an adult, a transgender may choose to change his physiology by taking female hormones to enlarge his breasts or by undergoing major reconstructive surgery to create a completely female body. He may then choose to identify himself as a "she" in society and even on legal documents. The process of becoming a transgender may take years. Many "sex-change"

Box 6.8   Cases to Role Play

Case 1 A 17-year-old girl comes in because she is depressed, and her mother is worried about her. The girl has begun a sexual relationship with a female basketball teammate, but claims that she still likes boys. The mother insists that her daughter is not a lesbian. The father will not have anything to do with his daughter if she chooses to date girls.

    Hint: Empathize with all about how difficult it is to deal with sexuality issues.
    Hint: Educate about the fact that a 17-year-old has not completely formed her identity.
    Hint: Educate about homosexuality, bisexuality, and heterosexuality (you may need to read up on these subjects).
    Hint: Focus on the cognitions underlying the mother's distress and the father's rejection.
    Hint: Talk with the daughter alone about the coming-out process.

Case 2 A 32-year-old man has been married for four years and has a two-year-old child. He had always thought that there was something different about him. He never really enjoyed sex with his wife, but does love her deeply. He also loves his daughter. Recently, he went to a bar and met a man with whom he felt a deep attraction. They went to the man's home and kissed. This is not his first time with a man this way. He started kissing men at age 18 but when he met his wife at age 25, he decided to try to be normal. He is scared that he is gay.

    Hint: Validate how difficult these types of thoughts and feelings are.
    Hint: Educate about coming out as a process.
    Hint: What is he scared about exactly?
    Hint: Educate that gays can still be parents.
    Hint: Explore the idea that he might not be gay. How can he find that out?

---

surgeons require that patients receive psychological assessment prior to this dramatic life change. Some transgenders do not undergo full sex-change surgery, as it is expensive. Instead, they live as women by dressing and grooming themselves as women and by taking hormones. Because this procedure is not common, most people in society have had little contact with transgenders. Most stereotypes about transgenders probably have to do with them being gay "drag queens" or "freaks." Human service workers will find transgenders to be fairly normal except that they are not happy living as the biological gender with which they were born. Some may be gay (attracted to men after sex-change surgery), and others may be attracted to women.

Chapter Review

The importance of cultural sensitivity in the field of crisis intervention is essential for effective management of a crisis. It is not an easy task, and most beginning counselors struggle with learning how to use the etic and emic issues presented by clients. Although no ethnic group is homogeneous in its makeup, there are certain emic characteristics of certain groups that when kept in mind, make the task of counseling more effective.

Correct Answers to Pre-Chapter Quiz

1.T   2.T   3.F   4.F   5.T   6.T   7.F   8.F   9.T   10.T

Key Terms for Study

African Americans: As seen by the crisis worker, a minority group that does not use the mental health system often. The historical roots of this group help explain why its members tend to resolve crises through the extended family and clergy rather than through governmental or other mainstream agencies. Racism and discrimination are still common problems for this group and must be kept in mind by crisis workers. Religion has historically been important in helping this group to get through the many daily stressors they encounter in America.

Asian Americans: As seen by the crisis worker, a minority group whose members may seek the services of mental health workers in crises, but who prefer a problem-solving approach similar to that used by a family doctor to treat physical illnesses. The crisis worker must be aware of issues of shame and obligation because they may come into play when a family member is in crisis. Crisis workers must also respect the family structure to prevent resistance to proposed coping alternatives.

Ataque de Nervios: A self-labeled syndrome found in Latinos in which they experience a misture of anxiety, panic, depression, and anger.

Catholicism: This is the primary religion of most Latinos and affects many aspects of their lives.

development of cultural sensitivity: A four-stage process during which counselors learn to consider cultural factors when they are conducting counseling sessions. The stages are (1) lack of awareness of cultural issues; (2) heightened awareness of culture; (3) realization of the burden of considering culture; and (4) beginnings of cultural sensitivity.

emic: This refers to behaviors and traditions particular to a certain cultural group.

emotionalism: This refers to the idea that Latinos tend to approach situations dramatically and by fully expressing feelings to others.

enmeshed: This type of family structure is noted for its focus on belonging, support, and lack of privacy and independence.

etic: This refers to behaviors and traditions of all or most humans regardless of race, ethnicity, or culture.

familismo: This idea refers to the focus latinos give to the family over all other relationships.

Hispanic: A term sometimes used to describe people who ethnic origins are based in Central and South America or Mexico.

Latino: An alternative term use to describe people whose family hold the traditions of Spanish speaking countries.

marianisma: This term describes the traditional Latina norm of being the self-sacrificing mother and wife.

machismo: This concept refers to the Latino males role as the provider and protector of his family to prove his virility.

Mexican Americans: As seen by the crisis worker, a cultural group whose members seek mental health services more often than African Americans or Asian Americans. Mexican Americans suffer crises related to language barriers, religious differences, and cultural differences in child rearing. Families tend to be enmeshed, and children are encouraged to be dependent.

personalismo: This refers to Latinos preference for relationships over tasks, and creating a sense of relating in more than a strictly business-like manner.

role of systems theory: An important element in working with clients from minority groups. The crisis worker must identify family roles and allowable behavior for a particular cultural group; these may be different from mainstream roles and behaviors. Imposing mainstream psychological theories on other cultures is often counterproductive.

Crises of Personal Victimization: Child Abuse, Elder Abuse, Intimate Partner Abuse, and Sexual Assault

_____ 1. Child abuse rates are less than 100,000 a year in the United States.

_____ 2. Spousal abuse only exists when couples are poor.

_____ 3. The main reason a battered wife stays with her batterer is fear.

_____ 4. Counselors are mandated to report suspected cases of child sexual abuse.

_____ 5. Rape trauma syndrome is a form of PTSD.

_____ 6. Child abuse accomodation syndrome includes secrecy.

_____ 7. Battered woman's syndrome is very rare amongst wives who are battered for more than 10 years.

_____ 8. Honeymoon is the first stage in the battering cycle.

_____ 9. Empowerment is an inapproporiate model for rape survivors.

_____ 10. Perpetrators of abuse often have very high self-esteem.

As was discussed in Chapter 9, personal threat can be a cause of **post-traumatic stress disorder (PTSD)**. This chapter deals with three very prevalent forms of personal threat that continue to occur in the United States and worldwide. The survivors of these forms of victimization frequently suffer from the delayed type of PTSD because they are prevented from or inhibited in seeking professional help. Unlike the victims of a natural disaster or a bombing, these victims are sometimes not believed and are blamed for the assaults against them. This leads to feelings of shame, guilt, and suppression of the victimization. Additionally, because these forms of victimization are often committed by family members and acquaintances, victims and their families have real reasons not to report the assault; namely, that they may be dependent on the perpetrator for survival. Lastly, and unfortunately, even when these forms of victimization are reported, the judicial system does not always provide justice for the victim, though judicial decisions in favor of victims have become much more common over the past 20 years.

Child Abuse

Child abuse may come to a crisis worker's attention in several ways. In each case, the person's feelings of shame, fear, guilt, and anger exist and need to be identified, so he or she can begin to understand the family or individual dynamics that led to the abuse. Once the person understands why and how the abuse occurred, there is hope that he or she can overcome the emotional trauma created by the abuse.

Prevalence

The National Center on Child Abuse Prevention Research (2005), a program of the National Committee to Prevent Child Abuse, estimates that in 2002 there were 1.8 million referrals alleging child abuse or neglect accepted by state and local child protective services agencies for investigation or assessment. These referrals included more than 3 million children, and of those, approximately 896,000 children were determined to be victims of child abuse or neglect by the child protective services agencies. In 2007, The National Child Abuse and Neglect Data system reported approximately 1,760 child fatalities caused by an injury resulting from abuse or neglect . The number and rate of fatalities have been increasing over the past five years. This might be attributed to improved data collection and reporting (Child Welfare Information Gateway, 2010). Of the the children who die due to abuse and neglect, 42.2 percent are younger than 1 year old, 33.5 percent are 1-3 years old, 12.9 percent are 4-7 years old and 11.2 percentare 8-17 years old. The U.S.

Department of Justice reported a total of 861,602 substantiated child abuse reports in 1998. Of these substantiated cases during that year, 461,274 were neglect cases; 195,891 were physical abuse cases; 99,278 were sexual abuse cases; and 51,618 were emotional abuse cases (U.S. Department of Justice, retrieved 11/04/01).

Did you know that:

- More than half of child fatalities due to maltreatment are not recorded as such on death certificates.
- 90 percent of child sexual abuse victims know the perpetrator in some way and that 68 percent are abused by family members.
- Child abuse occurs at every socio-economic level, across ethnic and cultural lines, within all religions and at all levels of education.
- 31 percent of women in prison in the U.S. were abused as children.
- Over 60 percent of people in drug rehabilitation centers report being abused or neglected as a child.
- About 30 percent of abused and neglected children will later abuse their own children.
- About 80 percent of 21 year olds that were abused as children meet the criteria for at least one psychological disorder.
- The estimated annual cost resulting from child abuse and neglect in the United States for 2007 was $104 billion! (National Child Abuse Statistics, 2010)

The discrepancy between reported cases and cases considered actual cases of child abuse by the judicial system could be the result of a variety of factors, such as false reporting, inaccurate reporting, or lack of evidence; also, children sometimes change their minds about reporting the abuse. Counselors are advised to be aware of the emotional ramifications of child abuse reports, whether substantiated or not. Even a false report could be a signal that a family is in crisis. The crisis worker can use the feelings and perceptions associated with both false and substantiated reports as a way to identify unmet needs and other problems in a family unit.

Sometimes the crisis interventionist will be called on to work with a child, the child's parents, or the entire family when a child is being abused by the parents. The abuse may or may not be the presenting problem. At times, a social worker will refer the family for counseling after a teacher or doctor reports the case to the district's child protective agency. In other cases, the crisis counselor may discover abuse to exist in a family that came in for other reasons. When this occurs, the crisis worker is mandated by law to report the case to the state's child protective agency.

Types of Child Abuse

Child abuse can be categorized into four types. **Physical abuse** occurs when damage to tissues or bones is inflicted on a minor by other than accidental means. Whenever parental discipline causes marks on a child, it is typically considered abuse. **Sexual abuse** occurs when an adult or individual several years older than the minor engages in any sexual contact. This can include intercourse, oral sex, anal sex, exhibition, fondling, or kissing. When a family member sexually abuses the minor, the contact is considered incest and is reported to child protective services. When the sexual abuse is perpetrated by someone other than a family member, the offender is usually dealt with by law enforcement. **General neglect** occurs when parents fail to provide for the minor's basic needs, such as food, shelter, clothing, and proper medical care. Society and the law expect a child to be properly supervised, fed, and protected from bad weather by clothing and housing. **Emotional abuse** is the hardest to prove, but probably the most prevalent type of abuse. In this type, a minor is repeatedly criticized and demeaned, receives no love or nurturance, and is not allowed to develop a sense of self. Parents who treat their children this way are usually the most psychologically disturbed of all types of child abusers, except perhaps for some sexual abusers.

How to Detect Child Abuse and Neglect

There are many clues for identifying child abuse and neglect. One sign alone may not necessarily indicate abuse, but if a number of signs are present, it is prudent to consider the possibility of abuse. Some signs that a child might be abused include:

- Is habitually away from school and constantly late; arrives at school very early and leaves very late because the child does not want to go home
- Is compliant, shy, withdrawn, passive, and uncommunicative
- Is nervous, hyperactive, aggressive, disruptive, or destructive
- Has an unexplained injury, a patch of hair missing, a burn, a limp, or bruises
- Has an inordinate number of "explained" injuries, such as bruises on arms and legs over a period of time
- Has an injury that is not adequately explained
- Complains about numerous beatings
- Complains about the mother's boyfriend doing things when the mother is not at home
- Goes to the bathroom with difficulty
- Is inadequately dressed for inclement weather; for example, is wearing only a sweater in winter for outerwear
- Wears a long-sleeved top or shirt during the summer months to cover bruises on the arms
- Has clothing that is soiled, tattered, or too small
- Is dirty and smells, has bad teeth, hair is falling out, or has lice
- Is thin, emaciated, and constantly tired, showing evidence of malnutrition and dehydration
- Is unusually fearful of other children and adults
- Has been given inappropriate food, drink, or drugs

A counselor might suspect abuse or neglect when a child exhibits several of these behaviors. These behaviors might be observed directly by the crisis worker or may be shared with the counselor by someone else who has seen these behaviors in the child.

In addition to observing signs in the child, a counselor may have the opportunity to observe parental behaviors and attitudes about the child. These often provide information to a counselor about a parent being abusive with a child. Some possible indicators that parents are being abusive are:

- Shows little concern for their child's problems
- Takes an unusual amount of time to seek health care for the child
- Does not adequately explain an injury the child has suffered
- Gives different explanations for the same injury
- Continues to complain about irrelevant problems unrelated to the injury
- Suggests that the cause of the injury can be attributed to a third party
- Are reluctant to share information about the child
- Responds inappropriately to the seriousness of a problem
- Are using alcohol or drugs
- Have no friends, neighbors, or relatives to turn to in crises
- Are very strict disciplinarians
- Were themselves abused, neglected, or deprived as children
- Have taken the child to different doctors, clinics, or hospitals for past injuries (doctor shopping)
- Are unusually antagonistic and hostile when talking about the child's health problems (Orange County Social Services Agency, 1982)

The San Francisco Child Abuse Council (1979) has identified specific indicators of physical abuse to watch for: bruises on an infant; bruises on the posterior side of a child's body; bruises in unusual patterns (belt buckle, loop from wire); human bite marks; clustered bruises; bruises in various stages of healing; burns from cigarettes or ropes; dry burns; lacerations of the lip, eyes, gum tissues, or genitals; possible fractures; absence of hair; bleeding beneath the scalp.

Prevalence of Child Sexual Abuse

Approximately 15 percent to 25 percent of women and 5 percent to 15 percent of men were sexually abused when they were children. Most sexual abuse offenders are acquainted with their victims: approximately 30 percent are relatives of the child, most often brothers, fathers, uncles or cousins; about 60 percent are other acquaintances such as friends of the family, babysitters, or neighbors; strangers are the offenders in approximately 10 percent of child sexual abuse cases. Most child sexual abuse is committed by men. Studies show that women commit 14 percent to 40 percent of offenses reported against boys and 6 percent of offenses reported against girls (Finkelhor, 1994; Gorey & Leslie, 1997). Most offenders who abuse pre-pubescent children are pedophiles (individuals who are only sexually attracted to children). Sexual abuse has several specific indicators. When one or more of these are present, abuse should be considered.

When a child displays any of the 4 presumptive behaviors indicating child sexual abuse presented below, it is assumed that he or she has been sexually abused. Of course, it is not up to a crisis worker to make that determination, but these behaviors are enough to warrant a child abuse report to Child Protective Services because they create suspicion. Suspicion is all that is required for a mandated reporter to follow through with a report. The four presumptive behaviors indicating child sexual abuse are:

1. Direct reports from children. False reports from young children are relatively rare; concealment is much more the rule. Adolescents may occasionally express authority conflicts through distorted or exaggerated complaints, but each such complaint should be sensitively and confidentially evaluated.
2. Pregnancy. Rule out premature but peer-appropriate sexual activity.
3. Preadolescent venereal disease
4. Genital bruises or other injuries. Remember that most sexual abuse is seductive rather than coercive and that the approach to small children may be nongenital. The presence or absence of a hymen is nonspecific to sexual abuse.

In addition to these presumptive behaviors, there are a variety of other signs that a child may be or may have been sexually abused. If there are enough of these behaviors observed or described by the child or another in that child's life, a crisis worker may be suspicious of abuse and therefore required to make a report to Child Protective Services. Some other possible Indicators of child sexual abuse are:

1. Precocious sexual interest or preoccupation
2. Indiscreet masturbatory activity
3. Vaginal discharge; more often masturbatory or foreign body than abusive
4. Apparent pain in sitting or walking. Be alert for evasive or illogical explanations. Encourage physical examinations.
5. Social withdrawal and isolation
6. Fear and distrust of authorities
7. Identification with authorities. Too-willing acquiescence to adult demands may represent a conditioned response to parental intrusion
8. Distorted body image; shame, sense of ugliness, disfigurement
9. Depression
10. Underachievement, distraction, daydreaming
11. Low self-esteem, self-deprecation, self-punishment, passiveness
12. Normal, peer-appropriate behavior. Children may show no signs and carefully avoid risk of detection. (Orange County Social Services Agency, 1982)

Infant Whiplash Syndrome In the past couple of decades, a potentially life-threatening injury to children has been identified and described: **infant whiplash syndrome**, or **shaken baby syndrome**. It is a serious injury, and the results can be devastating.

Most of the time, infant whiplash syndrome occurs when adults become frustrated and angry with a child and shake the child. Most people are not aware how seriously this can hurt a child. Children have received whiplash injuries at other times also, such as at play and in car accidents. Such an injury can be sustained when anxious adults try to wake a child who is unconscious after a fall or a convulsion.

Young infants have very weak neck muscles and only gradually develop the strength to control their heavy heads. If they are shaken, their heads wobble rapidly back and forth. The result can be somewhat like the whiplash injury an adult suffers in a car accident. Usually, however, the injury to the infant is much more severe. The back-and-forth vigorous movement of the head may cause damage to the spinal cord in the neck and bleeding in and on the surface of the brain. It is very important that parents and other adults know about this kind of injury and never shake an infant or child for any reason.

Association of Child Abuse with Posttraumatic Stress Disorder

If child abuse is not detected and brought to the attention of mental health workers, the abused individual often develops symptoms of PTSD following the abuse, symptoms that often continue into adulthood. The trauma of being abused often affects a person's functioning in work and personal relationships. Often, adults who were sexually abused as children (**AMACS, or adults molested as children**) may unwittingly repeat the abuse with their own children or perpetuate abuse on themselves. Suicide and substance abuse are commonly associated with these individuals as well. As children, denying the abuse helped in their daily survival, but as adults, denial often works against their surviving daily stress.

Many children who are repeatedly abused develop a condition referred to as **child abuse accommodation syndrome**. In order not to feel the emotional torment of being abused, neglected, and sexually abused, the child protects himself or herself by accepting the abuse and not fighting it. Abuse can continue for many years before it gets reported. Sometimes it is never reported, and victims die with the secret of having been a victim of abuse. When it does get reported, it is often by accident. The family is not ready psychologically to handle the disclosure and everyone goes into a crisis state. Table 10.1 describes the child abuse accommodation syndrome and the defenses used to maintain an abusive relationship.

Providing crisis intervention for abused children and their families is key in reducing the extent of damage done. If intervention comes early, many children will not have to suffer from delayed PTSD as adults, and the abused

TABLE 10.1 Child Abuse Accommodation Syndrome

Abuse	Child is physically, sexually, emotionally abused or neglected
Secrecy	The perpetrator asks or demands that the child not tell anyone
Accommodation	The child does not fight the abuse or demand to be treated better
Disclosure	The abuse somehow is mentioned to someone, often by accident
Suppression	The child recants his/her story of abuse, may be told to by perpetrator

All family members use defenses: dissociation, repressions, denial, minimization, externalization

children and their parents, siblings, and other relatives have the chance of salvaging some form of satisfying relationship.

Reporting Child Abuse

Mandated reporting of child abuse nationwide began after passage of the Child Abuse Prevention and Treatment Act in 1974. This federal legislation required every state to adopt specific procedures for identifying, treating, and preventing child abuse and to report the efficiency of these procedures to the federal Department of Health, Education, and Welfare.

Currently, all 50 states have **mandated reporting laws,** although the person required to report differs from state to state. Professionals who are involved with children, such as teachers, nurses, doctors, counselors, and day care workers, have become increasingly important in the detection and treatment of child abuse (Tower, 1996, pp. 13–14). Any professional who works with children must be knowledgeable about the mandated reporting laws in his or her state.

In most states, when a crisis worker suspects that abuse is occurring or has occurred, the worker must call the local child abuse registry or other welfare or law enforcement agency and report the information to a peace officer or social worker. Next, the worker usually submits a written report. Once the abuse is reported to the **child protective services agency,** a social worker becomes responsible for investigating the case. Most reports are unsubstantiated; that is they do not meet the criteria of abuse specified by law. Others result in referral for crisis intervention. The goal is to remove the risk from the child rather than remove the child from the risk. When child abuse is reported, parents often enter into a major crisis state and need intervention to get through the ensuing social services investigations, the judicial system process, and the reality of having a child taken out of the home. Most people are not prepared to deal with these things and need support and education to cope with them and continue functioning. When a report is false, the crisis state is even worse, and these parents are often in extreme distress. Many have tremendous fear that their child will automatically be taken away when a report of suspected abuse is made, so the crisis worker can help by educating the parents on the probabilities of this not happening.

When the child has been abused by someone other than a family member, the police are to be notified. In most states, this type of abuse becomes a criminal case, and children are usually not taken from the home unless it is determined that the parents cannot protect the child.

Interventions with an Abused Child

When a crisis worker suspects that a child may be a victim of abuse, the worker must first, as gently as possible, confirm the abuse, and second, treat the problem. An abused child is not likely to come right out and confess being abused, because the child has been taught not to tell. Some other reasons why an abused child might not tell anyone that he or she is being abused are:

1. The child is physically, financially, or emotionally dependent on the abuser.
2. The abuser has threatened the child's safety or that of another family member.
3. The child blames herself or himself for what happened.
4. The child has been taught that the good are rewarded and the bad are punished and therefore assumes responsibility for the assault.
5. The child fears that no one will believe her or him, either because the abuser is a known and trusted adult or because the child has no proof.
6. The child has been given the message that sexual issues are never discussed.
7. The child does not have words to explain what happened, and adults in the child's environment are not sensitive to what the child means.
8. The child totally blocks the incident from his or her memory because of the trauma of the assault. Colao and Hosansky (1983)

Crisis workers provide abused children with a very safe atmosphere and assure them that they will be protected by the counselor and other helpers who will be contacted. A helpful reframe is to point out that the child's parents just need guidance or help so they can learn better ways to discipline. If a young child is being sexually abused, the counselor can point out that "Mommy (or Daddy) is sick and needs professional help from a doctor to stop what she (or he) is doing." Another effective comment is to tell the child that "many other children go through this, and when the helpers get involved, usually things start getting better."

If the crisis worker believes that the parents, when they have the child alone, will coax him or her to deny the abuse, the worker should call the child protective agency and detain the child if possible. However, if the worker is going to continue working with the family, it is often helpful to reframe the reporting so it appears to be *for* rather than *against* the parents. To prevent outrage from parents, it is a good idea to have every client sign a form before treatment outlining the limits of confidentiality and mandatory reporting requirements. This can be used when informing them of a report.

Reframing for the abusing parents or for the spouse of a perpetrator can help reduce defensiveness also. A counselor can point out to the parents that they should be glad someone cares enough about their child to take the time and energy to protect her or him, even if the abuse doesn't really exist.

Educating the parent about the system is also very helpful. By explaining that the social services agency does not want to take their child if there is any other way to resolve the crisis, parents may feel less distrress. If, however, the parents are guilty of severe abuse, they may remain hostile. In these cases, it is better to lose a client and get protection for the child.

Reporting child abuse to the state protective agency can be reframed as opening a way the family can gain access to resources and services they might not otherwise get. Saying, "I need all the help I can get in serving you" might help reduce their defensiveness.

In cases of neglect, it is fairly easy to convince parents that the social services agency is there to teach or provide resources. In incest and severe physical abuse cases, parents are often more resistant, and they need classes, groups, and marital and individual counseling. Sometimes, these perpetrators may go to jail, which leads to different issues for the children, nonperpetrating parent, and incarcerated parent. Children may feel guilt; the nonperpetrating parent may suffer financially; and the incarcerated parent will experience loneliness. Counselors may need to deal with any or all of these various problems.

Play Therapy   Abused children respond well to play therapy, especially very young, preverbal children who don't often respond to verbal therapy. Their concrete rather than abstract mental capacities prevent them from benefiting from insight-oriented verbal therapy. In play, they can work out their feelings symbolically and unconsciously. Coloring, painting, molding clay, telling stories, and playing with dolls can help clear up nightmares, acting-out behaviors, and withdrawal behaviors. If the abuse was reported early enough, three to seven sessions of play therapy for a young child (age 4 to 10 years) may be all that is needed, providing that parents are supportive and the risk of further abuse is eliminated. Crisis workers should refer children to therapists with expertise in play therapy when it seems appropriate. Although crisis workers may not be trained to provide play therapy, they may be able to explain the purpose and process of play therapy to a child or parents and encourage participation in it.

Family Therapy   Sometimes, children need to confront their parents so the children can hear an apology and acknowledgment of responsibility. These sessions can also be used to set up contracts between parents and children. An abused child may feel less afraid to be around a perpetrating parent if he or she is assured that the parent has a nonabusive plan of action that the parent will follow during times of stress or just daily life, which has been and will be monitored by a third party (the therapist).

The Battering Parent

Counselors can work more easily with abusive parents if they have some idea of why the parents behave as they do. The Orange County Social Services Agency (1982) has developed an outline, adapted below, that attempts to explain the **battering parent**. Remembering this information may be helpful for crisis workers trying to empathize with batterers, who often repulse them.

Battering parents often share certain characteristics. They were often violently or abusively treated physically or emotionally, or both, as children. They had insufficient food. They often lived with dirt and disease. As children, they suffered repeated fractures, burns, abrasions, and bruises. They commonly experienced overwhelming verbal onslaughts. They knew sexual abuse by molestation, incest, or aberrant sexual acting out. They engaged in little two-way communication. They tend to repeat the same behavior with their children.

As children, they developed a deep loss of self worth and experienced intense, pervasive demands and criticism from their parents. They were convinced that regardless of what they did, it was not enough, not right, at the wrong time, or a source of irritation or disgrace to the parents. They never had the opportunity to work out their anger toward, and forgiveness of, the parents. These people tend to perpetuate those feelings into adulthood and are often lonely and friendless, whether living an active or a lonely life.

When confronted with suspicions of battery, some parents display these behaviors:

- They show little concern, guilt, or remorse for the child's battered condition.
- They are fearful or angry about being asked for an explanation of the child's injuries.
- They make evasive or contradictory statements about the circumstances of the mistreatment, whether emotional or physical battery.
- They place blame on the child for any injuries.
- They criticize the child and say little that is positive about him or her.
- They see the worker's interest in the child's injuries or problems as an assault on themselves and their abilities.
- They refuse to participate in treatment.
- They cooperate out of fear for themselves rather than concern for the child, while they try to conceal as much as possible.
- They don't touch or look at the child.
- They have unrealistic expectations of the child's capabilities and behavior, disregard for and minimization of the child's needs, and no perception of how a child can feel.

- They show overwhelming feelings of the child's worthlessness as well as their own worthlessness.
- They express guilt over or expectation of another failure, or both.

The family unit of which the battering parent is a part often has these characteristics:

- There is little communication and understanding among family members.
- The family unit is vulnerable to any and all stresses or ill winds.
- The family generally fails in problem solving.
- The family uses the child as a scapegoat for pent-up frustrations resulting from personal and marital conflicts.
- Parents demonstrate their frustrations by child abuse that is only rarely premeditated.(Orange County Social Services, 1982)

The crisis worker can reframe therapy to these people as an opportunity to correct their own behavior and do better for their children than their parents or others did for them. Providing parenting information and skills will be a part of crisis interventions. Many parents will for the first time be educated on how to talk rather than yell; restrict rather than hit; and understand rather than discipline. Learning new skills will empower them to be more effective parents and be more successful in getting their children to do what they want them to do.

They will learn how to have a social relationship rather than a functional parent-object relationship. Giving them specific alternative behaviors to use when stressed with a child is helpful. Some suggestions for battering parents when they feel like they might abuse their child are:

1. Call a friend or neighbor.
2. Put the child in a safe place and leave the room for a few minutes.
3. Take ten deep breaths and ten more.
4. Do something for yourself, such as play your favorite music, make a cup of tea or coffee, exercise, take a shower, read a magazine or book.
5. Change your activity into productive energy, such as shaking a rug, doing dishes or laundry, scrubbing a floor, beating a pan or pillow, or throwing away unwanted trash.
6. Sit down, close your eyes, think of a pleasant place in your memory. Do not move for several minutes.

Interventions for Adults Who Were Sexually Abused as Children

As mentioned earlier, many adults molested as children seek crisis intervention. Sexual abuse is often repressed so well by children that it may not be detected even by skilled clinicians. When sexual abuse started in early childhood, continued for years, and was accompanied by physical abuse, ritual abuse, or emotional abuse, the surviving child or adult may need long-term therapy. Crisis workers may be needed to provide short-term counseling for these people to help them through the crisis of remembering and having to deal with their parents, knowing what they now know. This moment often has an emergency quality to it, and the counselor must watch for suicide closely. Once the initial crisis state has begun to subside, the client may choose to continue in long-term therapy.

Other molestation survivors can respond well to participating in support groups and reading books designed for them. Crisis workers are encouraged to become familiar with books about the topic and refer them to clients.

Perpetrators of sexual abuse need a different intervention plan than battering parents. Typically, sexual abuse perpetrators abdicate their responsibility for themselves, feel victimized by the family, and lash out all at once. Perpetrators must take full responsibility for their actions and work to reclaim the parts of themselves that they have disowned (Caffaro, 1992). A male perpetrator often views his child as a substitute wife, caretaker, and sexual partner; these demands require far more emotional energy than a child has.

Although controlling the sexually abusive behavior may be the initial goal of crisis intervention, at some point the offender will have to focus on the origins of his problem. According to Caffaro (1992), sexually abusive behavior by a father stems from his relationship with his own father. This relationship can be characterized as one of physical abuse, neglect, rejection, and abandonment. Because his largely absent father frequently did not display tender emotions toward him, the perpetrating father must learn to develop empathy in himself. Belonging to a men's group can be helpful. The members can serve as substitute fathers and can mirror the man's growing sense of self as well as demonstrate how to bond appropriately with others.

The crisis worker would do well to help this father express feelings of shame, fear, anger, and guilt in an accepting climate. Then, groups need to be created that focus on early childhood relationships with the man's father and his need to express his feelings and develop his sense of self. Although women sometimes sexually abuse children, it is more common for men to do so.

Elder Abuse

According to the National Center on Elder Abuse (1994), this abuse can be categorized as domestic elder abuse, institutional elder abuse, and self-neglect or self-abuse. Domestic elder abuse refers to mistreatment by someone who has a special relationship with the elder; it includes physical abuse, sexual abuse, emotional abuse, neglect, and financial or material exploitation. Most states collect data on these types of abuse and have mandatory reporting laws. Institutional abuse refers to the same types of abuse when they occur in residential facilities for elders, such as nursing homes and board and care homes. Self-neglect refers to elders' abuse or neglect of themselves, often because of mental impairment, that threatens their health or safety.

One of every 20 older Americans may be victims of abuse each year; nearly 1.57 million older people became victims of domestic elder abuse during 1991 (National Center on Elder Abuse, 1994). A survey of 30 states in 1991 reported the following types of elder abuse, with percentages of occurrence: physical abuse, 19.1 percent; sexual abuse, 0.6 percent; emotional abuse, 13.8 percent; neglect, 45.2 percent; financial exploitation, 17.1 percent; other types, 4 percent (National Center on Elder Abuse, 1994). The crisis worker needs to understand why some caretakers abuse the elderly. Crisis intervention may focus not only on helping the victim but also on helping the abuser, who is probably a caregiver.

Stress in the caregiver is often a cause of abuse. Dealing with elderly people who are mentally impaired is frustrating, especially for caregivers without proper equipment or skills. If this is the case, the crisis counselor may refer the caregiver to a support group, offer education about mental impairments, or help the caregiver find low-cost medical equipment. Respite care may be very useful for some caregivers. It gives them a break, allowing them to have a vacation from caregiving while a paid caregiver comes to the residence and cares for the elderly person.

In some facilities, the elderly can be kept for the entire day. The crisis counselor often helps the caregiver work through guilt feelings caused by the sense of abandoning the elderly relative. A useful reframe is to suggest that without getting a break, the caretaker is abandoning the elder in other ways, such as emotionally. A really loving husband, wife, or child would take a break in order to be refreshed and offer appropriate caregiving.

Remember that caregivers have other life stressors to deal with, and they may be taking out their frustrations on the elder because the elder is an easy target. If this is the case, the crisis worker can help caregivers cope better with life problems; these issues should be addressed as part of crisis counseling.

In cases of physical abuse, some suggest that the cycle-of-violence theory holds, in that the children of the elderly parents were abused by them when they were children. They then act out their anger on the dependent elder parent because the use of violence has become a normal way to resolve conflict in their family. The crisis worker must help adult child caregivers address their own past history of child abuse to stop the cycle.

In some cases, the abuser has personal problems, such as substance abuse, financial problems, emotional disorders, or other addictions. Adult children with such problems are dependent on their elderly parents to support them and provide a home for them. This situation increases the likelihood of conflict and abuse. Many states provide training for caregivers; some hospitals have support groups for caregivers; and the state's adult protective agency may offer support services for caregivers. The crisis worker needs to be aware of what is available in the community.

Interventions with Abused Elderly People

Dealing with elder abuse is a multifaceted process. It includes interventions by physicians, social workers, nurses, psychiatrists, psychologists, and other professionals and paraprofessionals, all working together to protect and heal the damage done to the elderly person. The crisis worker must be knowledgeable about community support groups for abused elders and the array of supportive and protective services that are available.

Public guardianship programs, financial planning, and transportation are just a few of the services available to help the elderly be more autonomous and be taken care of by people who are closely monitored. Mental health providers can also use an empowerment model with the elderly, teaching them assertiveness skills and self-advocacy. The crisis worker can encourage the elder abuse victim to join with others in educating the public and elders about the prevalence of the problem so the elderly won't feel shame and guilt in coming forward with reports of abuse.

As with all forms of abuse, crisis counseling must be supportive as the person speaks, always validating the shame and pain of abuse but always later focusing on the survival aspect that allows the person to move forward.

Family counseling may be an option, especially if the abuser and the abused will continue living together after the abuse has been reported. This counseling may focus on airing and resolving resentments, improving communication, and defining roles and expectations.

Intimate Partner Abuse and Domestic Violence

An Historical Perspective

Many feminists have examined the beginnings of wife abuse in an attempt to understand this social problem. As part of a grassroots movement in the 1970s, women began to propose an alternative causality model for wife battering to that offered by traditional psychiatric theories. Battering became viewed as a social illness rather than the result of a man's or woman's individual psychopathology. Women, according to these pioneer feminists, have always been portrayed as subservient in the media and have been trained to be so by parents and men alike since ancient times.

As far back as 750 B.C., laws were written that sanctioned wife abuse, making a woman property and the husband responsible for her. A "rule-of-thumb law" existed until 1864 stating that a man was allowed to beat his wife so long as the stick he used was no wider than a thumb (Fenoglio, 1989).

In 1974, the first battered women's shelter was created in Minnesota. Since that time, about 700 such shelters have been established throughout the United States. This is not enough, but at least it is a start. Feminists are now proposing that more emphasis be placed on making the man leave the home, as he's the one with the problem, rather than sending the wife and children out to a shelter for safety (Woods, 1992).

Women in Western industrialized nations are more fortunate than those in certain South American countries, where wife battering is legally sanctioned. One example is the case of a Brazilian man who was acquitted of murdering his wife by using the defense of machismo. The blow to his honor from having to live with the fact that she had committed adultery was more than a man should have to bear, according to the rules of this male-dominated society.

Although it is against the law to batter one's spouse, it is sometimes difficult to press charges and secure justice even in severe cases of spousal abuse. In 1989, police officers in some states were given the right to press charges if they observed spousal abuse, even if the battered spouse did not press charges. This change of attitude came about in part because of recent acknowledgment of the **battered woman syndrome** (a type of PTSD), which often inhibits the battered partner from pressing charges. In 1994, a new bill was passed in California requiring health practitioners who are employed in a health care facility, clinic, or doctor's office and who have knowledge of a woman being battered by a partner to report this behavior to a law enforcement officer. The reason for external control is the relatively new idea that a battered woman cannot adequately make the decision to get out of the dangerous situation if she suffers from battered woman syndrome. An additional bill was also passed in California that requires applicants for several professional licenses to show that they have completed course work in spousal abuse. Since the terrorist bombing on September 11, 2001, what formerly had been referred to as a "terrorist threat" (a batterer threatening to kill his partner) was instead referred to as a "criminal threat" (Arambarri, 2005). Although a criminal threat does not physically harm a victim, it is a form of emotional abuse and often prevents a victim from leaving a batterer.

Since the murder of Nicole Brown-Simpson in June 1994, the entire nation has been alerted to the reality of spousal abuse. The famous O. J. Simpson trial may have precipitated the abundance of spousal abuse movies, talk show topics, and legislative proposals that came in the mid-1990s. A major change prompted by the Simpson case has been a focus on providing counseling services for the batterer. The obvious flaws in the judicial system have been looked at, and instead of simply ignoring a batterer's behavior, as in years past, funding is now available to help prevent repeat battering by requiring that the batterer go to diversion groups. In years past, people held many misconceptions about what occurs in a violent relationship. Some of these myths about spousal abuse are:

1. Battering happens only to minorities and in lower socioeconomic families. (Domestic violence occurs among all races and in all socioeconomic backgrounds.)
2. Women are masochistic and achieve unconscious satisfaction in being beaten.

(This antiquated concept has not been accepted for many years. If women liked being beaten, they wouldn't suffer from battered woman's syndrome, depression, and PTSD.)

3. The battered woman has a dependent personality disorder.
   (Not all battered woman demonstrate dependency traits. Many are self-sufficient and highly capable of self-care and autonomy. The batterer is often dependent on the partner.)
4. Battering is caused by alcohol and drug abuse.
   (Although substance abuse is correlated to violence, it is not always involved in domestic violence. There are many causes for battering.)
5. Batterers are mentally ill.
   (Although batterers certainly have anger and control issues, they do not necessarily meet the criteria for mental illness.) (Woods, 1992)

Prevalence of Intimate Partner Abuse

Physical assault against both women and men is astonishingly common in our country. In a survey conducted in 1995 and 1996 (Tjaden & Thoennes, 1998), 8,000 women and men were asked about their experiences of being assaulted in their lifetime. The results indicated a very high prevalence of physical violence in our society. Fifty-two percent of the women and 66 percent of the men stated they had been physically assaulted in their lifetime. The type of assaults ranged from being pushed, grabbed, or shoved; having hair pulled; being slapped, hit, kicked, bitten, choked, hit with an object, or threatened with a gun or knife; or having a gun or knife used on them. Although it may be true that men are assaulted more than women throughout their life, violence against women by a spouse or partner is more prevalent than it is for men. In fact, 25 percent of surveyed women, compared with 8 percent of men, stated that they had been raped or assaulted by a current or former spouse or partner.

It is widely accepted that violence against women is primarily partner violence, with 76 percent of the women reporting that a rape or physical assault was perpetrated by a current or former husband or partner, compared with 18 percent of the men. Additionally, women are significantly more likely than men to be injured during an assault.

Stalking is another form of violence against men and women. The victim feels high levels of fear at the thought of the former spouse or lover following and perhaps inflicting injury on her or him. About 8 percent of the surveyed women and 2 percent of the men said they had been stalked during their lifetime. It is estimated that 1 million women and 371,000 men are stalked annually in the United States.

Violence against women by a significant other is so prevalent in our country that many websites have been created to disseminate information about this topic. The National Women's Health Information Center through the Office on Women's Health in the U.S. Department of Health and Human Services (2000) offers a variety of services for Internet users. Its purpose is to increase awareness of the problem, sponsor research, and provide information about facts and statistics regarding violence against women. It defines domestic violence (intimate partner violence) as acts of violence against women within the context of family or intimate relationships that include physical abuse, psychological abuse, sexual assault, emotional abuse, isolation, and economic abuse. Facts about domestic violence include:

- Domestic violence is the leading cause of injury for American women ages 15 to 44 years.
- An estimated 1.1 to 4 million are victims of partner abuse per year.
- One in four women will be assaulted by a domestic partner in her lifetime.
- Nearly one-third of women report being physically abused by a husband or boyfriend.
- Thirty percent of female murder victims have been killed by their intimate partners.

(The National Women's Health Information Center through the Office on Women's Health in the U.S. Department of Health and Human Services , 2000)

Although battering of a male partner by a woman occurs, this is not discussed in this chapter. (Examine the current literature on abuse of males by their female partners to learn more about this phenomenon.) About 97 percent of partner abuse cases are male to female battering. It is these cases that will be the focus of this section. Additionally, partner violence occurs in gay and lesbian couples. The reader is encouraged to refer to literature about this specific type of intimate partner violence.

How Are Children Affected?

Each year an estimated 3.3 million children are exposed to violence by seeing a family member abuse their mother or female caretaker (American Psychological Association, 1996, p. 11). Children are more likely to be abused themselves in homes where partner abuse occurs (U.S. Department of Justice, 1993). Although not all men who abuse women also abuse children, about 40 to 60 percent of men who abuse women also abuse children (American Psychological Association, 1996, p. 80). Sadly, when children are killed during a domestic dispute, 90 percent are under the age of 10, and 56 percent are under the age of 2 (Florida Governor's Task Force on Domestic and Sexual Violence, 1997, p. 51).

Why Do Women Stay?

You can probably make a few guesses why a woman would stay with a man who verbally, emotionally, physically, or sexually abuses her. Each woman being abused stays for her own reasons. Crisis counselors explore those reasons with the woman and help her understand that while she may be enduring the abuse for good reason, there is help available so that she doesn't have to continue living with the abuse. Some reasons why a woman might stay in an abusive relationship include:

- She is afraid that he'll kill her, the pets, her children, her family. He often threatens to do this.
- Her religious beliefs forbid her leaving (til death do us part).
- She is influenced by the profamily society (stay together at all costs).
- She is economically dependent on the man. He often has forced her to quit school or her job, or never allowed her to work or know about their finances.
- She has no resources (no place to go, no transportation, no money).
- The children need a father.
- She gets no support from her family; many of these women are told to stick it out.
- She hopes he'll change because she loves him when he's not abusive.
- She believes him when he says it is her fault he beats her.
- She sees no other options.
- She feels insecure and unable to take care of herself (psychological dependence).

The Battering Cycle

Spousal abuse can be understood as a recurrent three-phase pattern. According to Woods (1992), the **battering cycle** usually starts out in the honeymoon phase, proceeds through the tension building phase, moves onto the explosive stage, and returns to another honeymoon phase. At some point, over many years, the second honeymoon stage disappears and the relationship is based on a tension-explosion cycle. Table 10.2 describes this cycle.

Battered Woman Syndrome

After this pattern has been experienced for more than a couple of cycles, the woman often develops battered woman syndrome. This is a type of PTSD that needs to be addressed and treated by the crisis counselor. The three components of battered woman syndrome are:

1. **PTSD Symptoms:** Because of the traumatic effects of victimization by violence, various symptoms develop, as this violence is outside the range of normal human experience. The woman may re-experience the trauma in dreams, avoid stimuli associated with the trauma, avoid feelings, and experience a numbing of general responsiveness. She may be detached, experience loss of interest, show increased arousal and anxiety, and have difficulty sleeping.
2. **Learned Helplessness:** A state of learned helplessness develops after she attempts to leave or get help and meets with no success because of system failure or other factors. She defends against this frustration by learning to survive rather than by escaping the battering.

TABLE 10.2 The Battering Cycle

Stage	Woman	Man	Dynamics
Honeymoon Phase	Feels special, love, dependent	Jealous, overpossessive, love, dependency	Lack of mutuality, lack of healthy intimacy
Tension-Building Phase	Walks on eggshells, tries to prevent violence	Minor incidents, criticizing, yelling, blaming, may still feel in control of himself, tension is strong	Woman believes it's her fault that he's upset. Both may see that there is a problem. Window of opportunity for preventing next stage through intervention by counselor.
Explosive Phase	If she survives, often has bruises and broken bones, may end up in a hospital. Focus on survival versus escape.	Out of control, may terrorize wife for hours, break things, hit, spit, push, choke, burn, tie up, rape, or kick her.	Violence gets worse over time, sometimes police is called. Window of opportunity exists for woman before denial sets in.
Honeymoon Stage Again	In shock, vulnerable to accepting apologies and flowers, hopes it won't happen again.	Apologizes, swears it'll never happen again, encourages her to go shopping, throw a party, treats her well for a while.	False resolution based on denial and minimization, life goes on. Tension reoccurs and the cycle continues. Honeymoon is the first stage to go until eventually, it consists of just tension-explosion.

3. **Self-Destructive Coping Responses to Violence:** Because she may perceive that her only choice is to stay (she may fear getting killed or has no place to go), she often uses drugs and alcohol to escape or may attempt suicide; at least, electing to die would be her choice (Fenoglio, 1989).

After determining that a client is a battered woman, a counselor can attempt to understand the phenomenological view of the woman without judging her. It may be helpful for you to have an idea of some of the beliefs these women have based on previous cases of counselors working at battered women's centers and shelters. Woods (1992) says that many of these women were brought up to take care of men and believe it is their role to nurture their partner when he's hurt.

Also, the woman may have been convinced by books, the media, or other mental health professionals that she is a co-dependent and is the sick one for deciding to stay. Rather than acknowledging that women in our society are socialized to be dependent, she may be judging herself and calling herself weak for staying.

Other women may not even be aware they are in an abusive relationship, and you may have to ease the client into accepting this idea and giving up denial. When a counselor begins to suspect that a client may be in an abusive relationship, it may be appropriate to explore various behaviors she has experienced with her partner. The list below presents various behaviors, feelings, dynamics that are typical in relationships when a woman is being battered and abused. Crisis counselors may use this information to guide their questions with a woman to ascertain whether she is being abused. These behaviors may also be used to educate the woman about typical patterns experienced by other women going through what she has been going through which might serve the purpose of validating and normalizing her experiences. If she has experienced many or most of these patterns, she is most likely in a battering relationship and educating her about the cycle of abuse and battered woman's syndrome may also be helpful. Some typical patterns seen in abusive relationships follow.

The partner has:

- Ignored her feelings
- Ridiculed or insulted women as a group
- Ridiculed or insulted her most valued beliefs, religion, race, heritage, or class
- Withheld approval, appreciation, or affection as punishment
- Continually criticized her, called her names, shouted at her
- Humiliated her in private or public
- Refused to socialize with her
- Kept her from working, controlled her money, made all decisions
- Refused to work or share money
- Took car keys or money away from her
- Regularly threatened to leave or told her to leave
- Threatened to hurt her or her family
- Punished or deprived the children when angry at her
- Threatened to kidnap the children if she left
- Abused, tortured, or killed pets to hurt her
- Harassed her about affairs he imagined she were having
- Manipulated her with lies and contradictions
- Destroyed furniture, punched holes in walls, broke appliances
- Wielded a gun in a threatening way

Thoughts or questions that the woman may have had:

- Does she often doubt her judgment or wonder if she is crazy?
- Is she often afraid of her partner and does she express her opinion less and less freely?
- Has she developed fears of other people and tend to see others less often?
- Does she spend a lot of time watching for her partner's bad, and not-so-bad, moods before bringing up a subject?

- Does she ask her partner's permission to spend money, take classes, or socialize with friends?
- Is she frightened of her partner's temper?
- Is she often compliant because she is afraid to hurt her partner's feelings or is afraid of her partner's anger?
- Does she have the urge to rescue her partner when or because her partner is troubled?
- Does she find herself apologizing to herself or to others for her partner's behavior when she is treated badly?
- Has she been hit, kicked, shoved, or had things thrown at her by her partner when he was jealous or angry?
- Does she make decisions about activities and friends according to what her partner wants or how her partner will react?
- Does she drink or use drugs? (Southern California Coalition on Battered Women, 1989)

Intervening with Battered Women

The purpose of intervention with a battered woman is to encourage her to act for her own well-being and safety. The five goals of intervention with a battered woman are these:

1. Let her know help is available.
2. Give her specific information about resources.
3. Document the battering with accurate medical records.
4. Acknowledge her experiences in a supportive manner.
5. Respect her right to make her own decisions.

While you are helping her identify the battering and her perspective, you will also be offering her your knowledge of battering and reframing some of her ideas. In addition, the crisis worker will offer empowering and supportive comments as well as suggest resources such as books, shelters, or groups.

Education Woods (1992) believes it is also important to give the woman various facts about battering presented at the beginning of this section. This will help her see she is not alone. She needs to be told as well that the violence usually increases in intensity and frequency and that her batterer needs professional help if he is ever to change.

Reframes Woods (1992), like most feminists working in the battered women's movement, believes that someone needs to tell the woman that the batterer has the problem and nothing she can do will prevent the next battering episode. This goes against the woman's belief that if she only had dinner ready, had the kids quiet, made the bed, and so on, he wouldn't get upset. Pointing out to her that he is sick and needs help from a professional may be accepted by her.

Another reframe has to do with her belief that she is weak for staying and for using drugs and alcohol. The crisis worker might reframe these behaviors as evidence of strength. Her behavior can be equated to that of a prisoner of war who learns how to get what he or she needs to survive. Her weakness is now strength. This new perspective can often turn her perspective around, so she starts to believe that she has strength to take new action with the crisis worker's support.

Cusick (1992) also agrees that the "therapist must show the client that she has orchestrated her own survival and has the skills to continue to do so" (p. 48).

Empowerment and Support   The last thing the battered woman needs is for someone else to make decisions for her about what she should do. The crisis worker may find it very stressful *not* to make decisions, because often the battered woman client will choose to stay with her batterer and be abused again. Crisis workers must pay attention to their own frustrations and feelings of helplessness with this population. It is easy for a counselor to fall prey to secondary PTSD while working with clients who have been assaulted repeatedly. Remember to consult with other counselors when you become aware of these feelings.

Typically, a battered woman has had every decision made for her by the batterer, so the best thing the counselor can do is provide her with choices and support them. The counselor can give her names, phone numbers, and suggestions. The woman's main concern will often be "How am I going to be safe?" The counselor may let her know she is most at risk when she leaves her batterer but that if she wishes, a plan can be made that will ensure her safety.

Helping her explore her own resources, such as family, friends, or church associates, is a good idea before you offer your own ideas. Battered women's shelters are usually free and should be used as a last resort. They are not like resort hotels, and a considerable amount of freedom is lost in a shelter. However, if there is nowhere else to go or no funds, the shelter is a great resource.

Following is an outline presented by Judy Bambas, volunteer coordinator at the Women's Transitional Living Center, on how to provide effective support for a battered woman:

1. Let her know you believe her.
   "Many women have been beaten by their partners."
   "I'm glad you've told me about the abuse."
2. Let her express her feelings. She has a right to be angry, scared, and so on. This may be the first time she is feeling safe enough to express anger over the abuse.
   "You seem very afraid of your partner."
   "You seem nervous talking about being abused."
   "You seem very angry about being abused."

3. Express your concern for her safety and the safety of her children. She may deny that abuse occurs or deny the level of danger to herself or her children.
   "This injury shows you are in great danger. You have a right to be safe."
   "Your safety is important. I'm very concerned about you and your children."

4. Let her know that help is available. Keep information at hand to share with her about help lines, shelters, counseling, and other resources. Ask her if she wants to report the abuse to the police. Explain slowly and carefully the choices available to her. She may need time and a safe place before she makes any decisions.
   "I have information that can help you."
   "There are many people in the community who can help you."

5. Reinforce the idea that nobody deserves to be beaten. She tends to believe some of the myths about domestic violence even though they may contradict her own reality. Remind her that she is not the cause of the beatings.
   "No one deserves to be hit."
   "You aren't the reason he hits you."

6. Realize that she may be embarrassed and humiliated about the abuse. She may worry that those who have offered to help in the past (e.g., family and friends) will be too burned out to help this time. Support her desire for help now.
   "You may feel embarrassed, but there are many women who have told me they are abused."

7. Be aware of the effects of isolation and control through fear. The woman may be physically or socially isolated, or both, due to location, language, intimidation, economic dependence, and other factors. Remind her that she is not alone. Connecting with others, through services such as support groups, can help break the isolation that battered women experience. Support her efforts to reach out to others.
   "You are not alone. Others can help and understand. I have information that may help you."

8. Assure her that you will not betray her trust.
   "What you share with me is confidential. My concern is for your safety."

9. Document the battering with specific information in her medical record. Her medical records may be used as evidence if she decides to press charges against the batterer. Be specific in description and sites of injuries. If the patient says that abuse is the source of the injuries, note, "Patient stated...," then continue the statement with who injured whom with what. If the patient refers to an instrument or weapon used by the abuser, note that in her record. If the injuries are inconsistent with the patient's explanation, make a note of it. If you suspect battering but the patient denies it, note "suspected abuse" in her record. Your notes may help identify her as battered on a future visit.

10. Remember that she may have other problems that demand immediate intervention. She may lack food or housing or be unable to care for her children or herself. Make appropriate referrals. If she is staying in a hospital, she may fear that the batterer will visit her. She may want her location to be kept confidential.

"It seems you have a concern about housing. I have information about other resources."

The Batterer

Is there ever hope for a batterer? Can he be cured? Can marriage counseling help? The answers to these questions are tricky because they depend on the man and his motivation. According to Woods (1992), there is only a 1 percent success rate for batterer treatment programs. Despite this very low estimate, some studies do show that court-ordered counseling may help.

A 1990 outcome study compared 120 court-referred abusers with a group of 101 nonreferred abusers. Results indicated that 75 percent of court-referred men who attended court-sponsored counseling reduced their recidivism rate. Another 1990 study found that after counseling, abusive men had not committed violent acts for one year. Based on these studies, the Family Service Center of the Marine Corps in San Diego established a model program to combat domestic violence (Barnett & LaViolette, 1993, pp. 126–127).

Other studies have suggested that short-term (6 to 12 weeks) psychoeducational batterer-intervention programs have helped some batterers to stop physical violence in the short term but were inadequate in stopping abuse over time. Some of the batterers even became more sophisticated in their psychological abuse and intimidation after attending such programs (American Psychological Association, 1996, p. 85).

More and more battered women's shelters are including batterers' programs in their facilities. Many more therapists are offering groups for this population, who really need the help. Judges are mandating counseling instead of jail time when a man is charged and convicted of battering his partner, a trend that demonstrates a greater focus on the man's part in the problem.

Arambarri (2005) suggests that these groups should focus more on power and control rather than anger management. Many times these batterers are referred to anger management groups led by therapists who are not specifically trained in domestic violence. She believes that unless the power and control issues are dealt with, the batterer may not be dealing with the real problem.

The alternative to counseling and jail may be a restraining order, by which the man is prohibited from physical proximity to the woman. However, recent statistics indicate that more than two-thirds of the restraining orders obtained by women against intimates who raped or stalked them were violated, and approximately one-half of the orders obtained by women against intimates who physically assaulted them were violated (U.S. Department of Justice, 2000). Although protection orders are a good idea, they aren't sufficient in preventing further violence. It would seem then that counseling is still an essential aspect of domestic violence prevention.

A Phenomenological View of the Batterer   It is possible that crisis workers will on occasion interview a batterer. This man may or may not see himself as a batterer, may or may not have chosen to seek help, and may or may not be amenable to intervention, depending on his personal and social resources. If a man somehow lands in a counselor's office (perhaps brought in by his partner or for a seemingly unrelated issues) and the crisis worker begins to suspect that battering may be an issue in the home, there are various factors that can aid the counselor and the client in recognizing that he is an abusive partner. Counselors are encouraged to proceed slowly and carefully when questioning these men in order to lessen resistance to intervention and to reduce denial when possible. Below is a list of characteristics typical of battering partners that counselors may consider asking about when ascertaining whether the suspected partner is abusive. The counselor might ask the person being abused if many of these qualities exist in the suspected abusive partner. Once the woman or the man sees how many of these qualities exist, they may be able to see the reality of the abusive relationship. Some of the personal characteristics of batterers are:

- They are very jealous.
- They sulk silently when upset.
- They have an explosive temper.
- They criticize and put down their partner a lot.
- They have difficulty expressing their feelings.
- They drink or use drugs.
- They believe that it is the male role to be in charge and have contempt for women.
- They are protective of their partner to the point of being controlling.
- They are controlling of their partner's behavior, money, decisions.
- They have broken things; thrown things at their partner; hit, shoved, or kicked their partner when angry.
- They were physically or emotionally abused by a parent.

Interventions with the Batterer

Woods (1992) describes many of the patterns battering husbands used to maintain power and control. Interventions both in group settings and individual sessions focus on educating these men about these patterns and how to stop them. Some behaviors used to maintain power and control are:

Intimidation: Putting her in fear by using looks, actions, gestures, a loud voice, smashing things, destroying her property.

Isolation: Controlling what she does, who she sees and talks to, where she goes.

Emotional abuse: Putting her down or making her feel bad about herself; calling her names; making her think she's crazy; using mind games.

Economic abuse: Trying to keep her from getting or keeping a job. Making her ask for money; giving her an allowance; taking her money.

Sexual abuse: Making her do sexual things against her will; physically attacking the sexual parts of her body; treating her like a sex object.

Using children: Making her feel guilty about the children; using the children to give messages; using visitation as a way to harass her.

Threats: Making or carrying out threats to do something to hurt her emotionally; threatening to take the children away; threatening to commit suicide; threatening to report her to welfare.

Using male privilege: Treating her like a servant; making all the big decisions; acting like the master of the castle.

Physical abuse: Twisting, biting, tripping, pushing, shoving, hitting, slapping, choking, pushing down, punching, kicking, using a weapon, beating, grabbing.

After educating a man on the destructive patterns he is using, a counselor might attempt marital counseling where they could try to work on communication skills and compromise, as is done with other couples. However, this approach doesn't always work if the man is extremely angry, paranoid, using drugs, or holds rigid beliefs about his rights as a man. When a crisis counselor begins to experience that, short-term crisis management is not effective, and other interventions will be necessary.

In fact, most feminists and clinicians who work in the field of domestic violence believe that traditional family therapy is not an appropriate intervention in domestic violence cases (Segel-Evans, 1991). They believe that the batterer is completely responsible for the violence, and that he should be the one in therapy to work on his violence problem. Marriage counseling gives him the message that his wife has a part in creating the violence, thereby exonerating him from full responsibility for his sickness. With this perception, the recommended treatment for domestic violence cases is twofold. First, the woman should be assessed for safety and given choices and support. It should be emphasized to her that her symptoms evolved only after the trauma of being abused. Second, the man should be the one to leave and attend groups for battering men or enter individual therapy, or both, to work on his violence. He must accept responsibility and learn more appropriate ways to communicate, deal with stress, conquer his insecurities, and learn to meet his own needs.

Not all clinicians agree with this perspective, however. Kugler (1992) agrees with many of the ideas but believes the battered woman is not the passive, helpless victim she is often portrayed to be. He holds the victim accountable for her own violence toward the husband, which may provoke his violence. Also, he believes therapists need to point out to the woman that the abuse won't stop unless she makes the man accountable—legally and morally. He suggests that mental health workers help empower the woman by assisting her to "realistically evaluate the situation and understand the interactional dynamics of the relationship" (p. 45). Then she can learn to alter her behavior, which may help alter his behaviors.

Kugler feels that too many women get weakened by well-meaning counselors who set the boundaries for them. This, he says, doesn't help the woman in the long run, for she is likely to enter another abusive relationship without having learned effective limit-setting behaviors.

Kugler does not believe that the woman gets blamed for the battering simply by understanding the abusive behavior in the context of the violence. He says that those who dogmatically say that couples' counseling is never an appropriate crisis intervention modality greatly limit help, especially for the woman who truly believes she has a part in the abuse and wants to work on changing her behavior.

As with all crisis work, counselors must keep all this information in mind as they interact with each client, using what will be helpful and putting aside parts that are not relevant.

Rape

Rape is the common term used when discussing sexual assault. It is a frequent form of assault in our society. Some of the clients who seek crisis intervention might have just recently been raped. Others will have been raped many years ago but have been motivated to come for help by a recent triggering event. For example, watching the Tyson trial brought out the anger of a 69-year-old woman who had been raped by her fiancée 40 years earlier (Heller, 1992). Victims of rape often go through similar stages called **rape trauma syndrome** (another type of PTSD). This syndrome is recognized in California courts as a condition that occurs following a rape. The crisis worker must help the rape victim proceed through these stages, which will be discussed later.

Like so many other common topics, rape has generated its own set of myths. Wesley (1989), a rape crisis counselor with the Orange County Sexual Assault Network, discussed a variety of myths and corresponding facts about rape. Crisis workers are encouraged to know the difference between fact and myth so that they may be better prepared to present a more realistic picture about sexual assault to victimized clients. Some of these myths are:

1. *Myth:* Rape is rare and will never happen to me.
   Fact: Every 6 minutes a rape takes place. The FBI estimates that 1 in 4 women and 1 in 10 men will be sexually assaulted in their lifetime. Most rapes are not even reported.
2. *Myth:* Rape is about sexual desire.
   Fact: Sex has little to do with it. Sex becomes the weapon, the vehicle to accomplish the desired end result, which is to overwhelm, overpower,

embarrass, and humiliate another person. Also, looking at typical rape victims shows clearly that this crime is not about sex: Ninety percent of disabled women will be raped. Children and the elderly are also at high risk of being raped because of their vulnerability. An attacker can easily overpower these victims.

3. *Myth:* Only strangers commit rape. Forced sex among acquaintances is not rape.

   Fact: In 60 to 80 percent of rapes, the victim and the assailant know each other. In addition, for women 15 to 25 years of age, 70 percent of the assaults are date rape. The woman is vulnerable at these ages because she is starting to have sexual feelings, set limits, and pursue intimate relationships.

4. *Myth:* Rapists are psychotic or sick men.

   Fact: Less than 5 percent of convicted rapists are clinically diagnosed as psychotic. The media present these cases to the public because of the bizarre nature of the rapes, but the rapist can be anyone.

5. *Myth:* Women who get raped are asking for it.

   Fact: Women who try to look attractive and sexy are asking for attention, approval, and acceptance—not victimization. Babies in diapers and fully clothed grandmothers being raped are evidence that rape is not caused by sexy clothes.

6. *Myth:* He can't help it; once he's turned on, he can't stop.

   Fact: Could he stop if his mother walked in? Humans can control their sexual behaviors. (Adapted from Wesley, 1989)

What Is Rape?

Rape is a sexual act against one's will; it is sexual violence. It might be intercourse, oral sex, anal sex, or penetration with any foreign object. Rape is a felony that carries a sentence of 1 to 16 years for each count. Most rapists don't go to prison because most rapes aren't reported. About 95 percent of rapists are men. Almost none of the men who are raped report it because of the perceived homosexual aspect of male-to-male rape. This is unfortunate because male rape victims underuse crisis services, leaving a population of men who will be struggling emotionally with feelings of humiliation and loss of masculinity. In a 1995 survey (U.S. Bureau of the Census), 1 out of 6 women and 1 out of 33 men has experienced an attempted or completed rape as a child or adult. Specifically, 14,903,156 women, and 1,947,708 men reported having been raped at some time in their life (Tjaden & Thoennes, 1998). An estimated 683,000 women are forcibly raped each year in the United States; that is, 1.3 women are raped every minute (Kilpatrick, Edmunds, & Seymour, 1992). Rape remains the most dramatically underreported crime; 70 to 84 percent of rapes are not reported to law enforcement.

Rape Trauma Syndrome

Rape victims often experience three identifiable stages after the assault; together, these stages comprise the rape trauma syndrome. This is the type of PTSD often seen in rape survivors. A crisis worker is well advised to understand these stages so as to better join with the client at any given point in the crisis.

Stage 1: *Immediate Crisis Reaction* During this acute phase, which lasts 2 to 6 weeks, the victim experiences emotional pain, specific physical pain, and general soreness. As with PTSD, sleep disturbances are common. The person often feels vulnerable when asleep or is fearful of nightmares. Eating disturbances will also be seen, evidenced by nausea and loss of appetite. Emotional reactions encompass hysteria, fear, anxiety, humiliation, shame, embarrassment, guilt, anger, and an acute sense of vulnerability. How the victim copes has a lot to do with her previous coping style.

Stage 2: *Reorganization* As the initial feelings start to subside, victims realize they may get through it. They may tell themselves they need to get back to normal and can't keep dwelling on the attack. This type of thinking leads to a state of denial whereby the experience is minimized or blocked altogether.

If victims don't get professional help, they may stay stuck in this phase. They may be able to function somewhat, but it will be at a lower level than before the rape. Mood swings, depression, psychosomatic illnesses, substance abuse, phobias, failed relationships, sexual dysfunctions, suicide attempts, and revictimization may be part of this phase. The crisis worker is likely to encounter victims who have been stuck in this phase for several years because they just can no longer function.

As discussed in Chapter 1, it is easier to work with victims who are in Stage 1 because they haven't invested energy in denial yet. The longer they wait, the longer the intervention will have to be.

Stage 3: *Reintegration* In reintegration, clients move from being victims to being survivors. With proper crisis intervention, they can emerge as stronger, more assertive persons, more aware of themselves and with increased self-esteem. After all, they have survived an extremely traumatic experience—evidence of their strength (Wesley, 1989).

Interventions with a Rape Victim

Much of the material about how to work with rape victims originally came from literature produced by the Orange County Sexual Assault Network (OCSAN). What follows is an integration of that agency's treatment approach to sexual assault with the ABC model presented in this book.

If rape victims contact a crisis worker immediately after the rape, they are likely to be confused about what steps to take. They may feel guilty and not consider themselves a victim who has the right to medical attention and police assistance (Heller, 1992). A counselor can help survivors decide what to do by providing information and resources. Overall, an **empowerment model** is suggested with this population. It encompasses the steps described next.

The Empowerment Model with Sexual Assault Survivors

A: Achieving Contact During the first 5 minutes or so, survivors are probably sizing up the crisis worker and thinking, "Can this counselor handle what I've got to say?" It is important for the helper to be calm, clear, and trustworthy and somehow convey the message, "I'm not going to be shocked."

During this early contact, counselors should reassure and validate clients for seeking help. Asking questions to get a clear picture of what happened helps to get the interview moving and calms clients. At this point, it isn't important to attain a full graphic picture of every detail. Reflecting, paraphrasing, and asking open-ended questions are excellent strategies for this stage.

Assessing for symptoms is also important in case a client needs help from a physician. Sometimes a client will be severely depressed and needs medication to function at even a minimum level.

B: Boiling Down the Problem to Basics At this point, it is appropriate to identify how clients are feeling now, keeping them in the present. To understand what makes the rape a crisis for them, a good question is this: "What is the hardest part for you?" The answer gives the counselor a place to begin, a focus for reframing, educating, empowering, and supporting the client. The statements following are models of the types you might find helpful at this time.

Supportive Statements Every rape victim needs to be believed and the experience legitimized. People rarely make up stories about being raped. Statements like the following will help to restore the victim's dignity and reduce his or her sense of embarrassment:

"It must have been frightening."

"It wasn't your fault; you didn't ask for this to happen and you deserve to be taken care of and treated with dignity and respect."

"It's difficult to scream when you're frightened."

"Sure, you were hitchhiking, but not in order to get raped."

Educational Statements Clients can benefit from learning about rape trauma syndrome. This information helps to normalize their experience so they don't think they're reacting unnaturally. Clients also benefit from knowing that rape is not about sex but about power. The rapist just happened to use sexual behavior as the weapon of assault.

Empowering Statements Constantly help clients focus on being in control of their decisions:

"You weren't in control during the assault, but now you are in control. You've already chosen to seek help from me. Let's look at some other options so you have more choices."

Reframing The crisis worker can offer a different way of interpreting victims' behavior while being raped. She can help clients see that in no way should they consider themselves stupid for not resisting the rapist.

"It sounds as though you were very wise to keep still and quiet rather than risk further injury by fighting."

C: Coping By exploring the ways clients have coped with other crisis situations, you can activate their strengths and further empower them. Encourage them to think of other ways to cope. Perhaps they can use their current support systems and reach out to such new systems as support groups.

After clients have presented all the ways of coping they can think of, the crisis worker can suggest other resources and brainstorm additional ways. The worker might recommend reading certain literature, taking a self-defense course, or calling a hotline; she might also offer to accompany the client to the police station or doctor's office. As long as the client makes the decision, many options are possible for the crisis worker.

One of the newer approaches to working with rape victims is EMDR (eye movement desensitization and reprocessing). Most communities have certified EMDR therapists who have had considerable success in helping sexual assault victims. EMDR therapy targets all of the information related to the trauma, allowing the cognitive elements and emotional elements to be reprocessed. Often, the end result is increased feelings of control and power. "Part of the treatment includes facilitating the emotional adoption of positive self-beliefs, such as 'I am now in control,' or 'I now have choices'" (Shapiro & Forrest, 1997, p. 135). This approach would appear to fit with the empowerment model previously discussed.

Date and Acquaintance Rape

Date rape refers to a situation in which a woman voluntarily goes out with a man and may even engage in some form of sexual conduct but at some point is overpowered by the man. It brings up some especially difficult issues because the woman is confused. At a certain point, she wanted to be with this person. However, when the situation gets out of control, she often doesn't know what to do. Women are most often date raped between 16 and 24 years of age. The peak rate of victimization occurs in the 16- to 19-year-old age group, with the next highest rate in the 20- to 24-year-old age group (Koss, 1992). About 90 percent of college women surveyed report that their attacker was a boyfriend, ex-boyfriend, friend, acquaintance, or coworker. Nearly 13 percent of the women surveyed reported being the victim of date rape, and 35 percent the victim of attempted rape while on a date (Fisher, Cullen, & Turner, 2000).

Steiner (1994), the clinical supervisor at Mariposa Women's Center in Orange, California, offers some valuable thoughts on how to educate and support women who are survivors of date rape or any woman at risk of date rape:

- First, no one can predict how [she] will react in a threatening situation. Nor can she blame herself for not reacting differently. Too much of a survivor's recovery is spent trying to redo what has already happened. We all can change only our future, not our past.
- Don't be afraid to be seen as rude or paranoid. If he gives you a hard time or humiliates you because you don't want to go into his room, or to his apartment, or for a drive, he is exhibiting a behavior common to date rapists—no respect for your feelings.
- Go ahead, wreck his stereo or anything else you can reach if he doesn't stop when you say no. When it's all over, he'll have a hard time saying, "You know you wanted it, and no one would believe you anyway" if his room is in a shambles. If somehow you were wrong about him, a new stereo is a lot cheaper than a year of recovery from rape.
- When you don't report it, and you don't tell your close friends, you increase the damage inflicted by the rape by isolating and blaming yourself. If your friends don't react the way you had hoped, don't blame yourself. Remember that what happened to you is bad, and they are afraid to believe it could happen to them. They need help in facing it.
- Everybody needs help in recovering from traumatic events. Ask for what you need from friends, family, rape support centers, and others trained to help.
- People do recover from rape, and they are never the same. They can be stronger, more compassionate to others, and more respectful of themselves.

Chapter Review

Personal victimization often leads to PTSD and other emotional problems. Whether it be child abuse, sexual assault, partner abuse, elder abuse, or any other form of physical assualt, people often benefit from crisis intervention. Child abuse accommodation syndrome, battered women syndrome and rape trauma syndrome have been seen in these type of assaults and can help survivors better understand what they are going through. Because these crises involve the legal system, crisis workers are encouraged to know the laws in their state relating to these situations. Empowerment is considered a vital intervention for all of these forms of victimization to help move the client from being a victim to a survivor.

Box 10.1   Cases to Role-Play

Case 1 A 14-year-old girl comes to this clinic because her mother believes something is wrong; her daughter's grades have been going downhill, and she does not like the people her daughter hangs around with at school. The girl's father has been having a sexual relationship with her since she was seven years old. She does not want to tell anyone because he threatened to throw her out of the house if she told. Her mother appears to be happy with him.

Case 2 A 47-year-old man, who is an elder at his church, comes to counseling. He runs his own business, which is very successful. He lives in a high-class neighborhood and everyone believes he is an ideal citizen and parent. He is raising three children on his own because his wife died two years ago. He has come in because for the last year he's been taking out his frustrations on his oldest child, who is nine years old. He has broken the boy's arms twice and has hit him with a board on several occasions. He realizes he needs help.

Case 3 A woman brings her family in because she and her spouse were reported for child neglect. She tells the interviewer that she is very upset by the false statement. She is a very religious person, and her children are very well taken care of. They eat at specific times and are not allowed to snack. During the interview, the children are going through the wastepaper baskets looking for food. The mother tells you that they missed breakfast this morning and will have to miss another meal because good children do not miss meals.

    Hint: Maintain a nonjudgmental attitude.

Case 4 A very upset 25-year-old woman comes to you. Her husband has threatened to kill her 4-year-old son. Her son is not the child of her husband. Last night her husband was drinking, and her son was bothering him. He hit the boy and gave him a black eye. It is the first time he has hit her son. Usually, he takes his frustrations out on her. She tells you not to tell anyone because she is afraid of what her husband would do if he found out that he had been reported.

Case 5 A 27-year-old nurse comes to you. She is working to put her husband through medical school. She is complaining about being unassertive. She sits uneasily in the chair. When she moves, she sometimes grimaces in pain. She loves her husband and wants to please him but does not think she can. Due to her lack of sexual responsiveness, he sometimes gets extremely angry and does things.

Case 6 A 65-year-old woman comes to you. She lives in a retirement trailer village with her husband, who is a retired salesman. She comes to the session crying. Her mouth is cut and her right eye is swollen and bruised. She expresses anger and hatred toward all men. Her husband beat her last night because there was too much grease on his plate. She wants to leave but is afraid. He has threatened to kill her if she tries to leave.

Case 7 A young woman who has recently been raped by an old friend comes to counseling. She went to a party and had a few drinks. The friend walked her to her car and then forced her into the car and raped her. She has told no one. Her biggest problem is that this friend works for the same company she does.

Case 8 A 32-year-old male was raped by two men. He is feeling a great deal of shame because he thinks he's the only male this has ever happened to. He is also very angry because he was unable to do anything to stop the rape. One of the men had a gun. He is afraid no one will believe his story. He feels that he might just end it all now because his life won't be worth living after this.

Case 9 A 19-year-old coed was walking across campus when four men forced her into their van and raped her. There were other people around when it happened, but no one did anything to stop the event. When she told her parents, they became upset with her and believed she was to blame. Her father told her that if she would just stop wearing such sexy clothes, these things wouldn't happen. She is confused and feels unable to study, and she has thoughts about suicide.

Correct Answers to Pre-Chapter Quiz

1.F 2.F 3. T 4. T 5. T 6. T 7.F 8. T 9. F 10.F

Key Terms for Study

AMACS (adults molested as children): Adults who often manifest PTSD because of the unresolved emotional residue of childhood sexual abuse. Support groups for this population are increasing.

battered woman syndrome: A form of PTSD frequently manifested by women who are continually beaten by their domestic partners. Often, the woman develops a sense of helplessness and hopelessness. She does not consider leaving her abuser; rather, she focuses on surviving the abuse. She is often in a daze.

battering cycle: The events leading to, through, and away from domestic violence. The cycle begins in the honeymoon period, when both partners are in love and feel happy. The tension builds and eventually an explosion happens, either verbally or physically. After the explosion, the batterer feels relieved and seeks forgiveness, and the honeymoon begins again. Eventually, the honeymoon period goes away, and the couple oscillates between tension and violence.

battering parent: Parent who beats a child as a disciplinary action, out of frustration, or for other reasons. This parent was probably abused as a child and lacks the skills to properly communicate with and discipline a child. The parent's anger is out of control, and the parent is using the child to relieve stress.

child abuse: One type of trauma that can cause PTSD (too prevalent in our society). The four most common kinds of child abuse are these:

Physical abuse: Indicated by tissue damage, broken bones, or organ damage from nonaccidental means. Burns, welts, bruises, and other marks are also indications.

Sexual abuse: Occurs when an adult gratifies himself or herself sexually with a minor. Abuse ranges from fondling to voyeurism to intercourse.

General neglect: Indicated when a parent or guardian fails to provide for a child's basic needs, such as food, shelter, clothing, and medical care.

Emotional abuse: Occurs when a child is continually humiliated, criticized, and deprived of love. Usually leads to severe psychiatric symptoms and is difficult to prove.

child abuse accommodation syndrome: A protective condition in which an abused child maintains secrecy about the abuse, permits it to reoccur, and, even if the abuse is accidentally disclosed, tries to suppress it.

child protective services agency: A county or state agency established to protect children from abuse by investigating reports of child abuse and intervening when necessary.

date rape: The most common form of rape for women between the ages of 15 and 24 years. While out with a friend or date, or while at a gathering with acquaintances, a woman is sexually assaulted. Often, the man does not realize he is raping her.

empowerment model: An intervention model for clients in crisis that helps to restore a person's sense of control. In working with survivors of rape, crisis interventionists use this type of approach when issues of power and feelings of helplessness are discussed. The survivor is presented with alternative ideas that help him or her feel more in control and powerful. The worker may want to point out choices and decisions that are still under the person's control, even though the sexual assault may not have been.

infant whiplash syndrome/shaken baby syndrome: A very serious form of child abuse that results when a baby is shaken. The shaking causes the brain to roll around in the skull cavity. This abuse can lead to brain damage or death.

mandated reporting laws: Laws requiring professionals such as counselors, teachers, and medical personnel who work with children to report any suspicions of child abuse to either a child protective agency or a law enforcement agency. Exactly who is required by law to report and the procedures for reporting vary from state to state.

posttraumatic stress disorder (PTSD): A state in which a person re-experiences a traumatic event as flashbacks or in nightmares, feels anxious and hypervigilant, and has impaired functioning.

rape trauma syndrome: A form of PTSD commonly found in women and men after a sexual assault. First, there is the immediate crisis reaction, with all the symptoms of anxiety one would expect. Then, the rape survivor attempts to reorganize. Without help, the survivor reorganizes by using ego defense mechanisms. With help, the survivor learns to cope with her or his feelings and works through the trauma to move to the third phase: reintegration. Finally, the survivor comes to terms with the assault and integrates it into his or her life.